STATE OF VERMONT
DEPARTMENT OF LIBRARIES
REGIONAL LIBRARY
RD 2   BOX 244
ST. JOHNSBURY, VT 05819

Robert B. Jackson's
Big Book
of
OLD CARS

Robert B. Jackson's
Big Book
of
OLD CARS

Henry Z. Walck, Inc.
A Division of
DAVID McKAY COMPANY, INC.
New York

Copyright © 1978 by Robert B. Jackson
ANTIQUE CARS © 1975 by Robert B. Jackson
CLASSIC CARS © 1973 by Robert B. Jackson
THE STEAM CARS OF THE STANLEY TWINS © 1969 by
Robert B. Jackson

All rights reserved, including the right to
reproduce this book, or parts thereof, in any
form, except for the inclusion of brief quotations
in a review.

Library of Congress Cataloging in Publication Data

Jackson, Robert B
Robert B. Jackson's Big book of old cars.

Includes index.
CONTENTS: Antique cars.—Steam cars.—Classic cars.
1. Automobiles—History—Juvenile literature.
2. Automobiles, Steam—Juvenile literature. [1. Automobiles—
History. 2. Automobiles, Steam] I. Title. II. Title: Big
book of old cars.
TL147.J34   629.22'09   78-5207
ISBN 0-8098-6025-2

10 9 8 7 6 5 4 3 2 1
Manufactured in the United States of America

OTHER BOOKS BY ROBERT B. JACKSON

BEHIND THE WHEEL: *Great Road Racing Drivers*
BICYCLE RACING
CARS AGAINST THE CLOCK: *The World Land Speed Record*
CHAMPIONSHIP TRAIL: *The Story of Indianapolis Racing*
EARL THE PEARL: *The Story of Earl Monroe* (Revised Edition)
FISK OF FENWAY PARK
"HERE COMES BOBBY ORR"
JABBAR, GIANT OF THE NBA
JOE NAMATH, SUPERSTAR
JOHNNY BENCH
QUARTER-MILE COMBAT: *The Explosive World of Drag Racing*
RACING CARS
ROAD RACERS: *Today's Exciting Driving Stars*
ROAD RACING U.S.A. (Revised Edition)
SOCCER: *The International Sport*
SPORTS CARS (Revised Edition)
SWIFT SPORT: *Car Racing Up Close*
WAVES, WHEELS AND WINGS: *Museums of Transportation*

Contents

I
ANTIQUE CARS

1	*The Appeal of Antique Automobiles*	3
2	*Automotive Pioneers*	7
	Duryea	7
	Oldsmobile	10
	Stanley	14
	Ford (Model T)	17
3	*Automobiles Become Big Business*	23
	E.M.F.	23
	Buick	25
	Maxwell	28
	Brush	32
	Briscoe	35
4	*The Automobile Age Arrives*	38
	Chevrolet	38
	Hudson	42
	Cadillac	45
	Packard	48
	Ford (Model A)	52
5	*Seeing Antique Cars*	56
6	*Antique Car Museums*	61

II
STEAM CARS

1	*F.E. and F.O.*	65
2	*Yankee Competitors*	76

3	*The Wogglebugs on Ormond Beach*	88
4	*End of the Road*	100

III
CLASSIC CARS

1	*Majestic Giants of the Past*	119
2	*Classic Cars from Abroad*	126
	FRANCE	126
	Bugatti	126
	Hispano-Suiza	129
	GERMANY	132
	Mercedes-Benz	132
	GREAT BRITAIN	134
	Rolls-Royce	134
	Bentley	137
	ITALY	140
	Alfa Romeo	140
	Isotta-Fraschini	142
3	U.S. Classic Cars	146
	Auburn	146
	Duesenberg	149
	Cord	151
	Stutz	154
	Packard	157
	Cadillac	159
	Lincoln Continental	162
4	*Seeing Classic Cars*	168
	Index	177

I
ANTIQUE CARS

Acknowledgment

The photograph on page 39 is reproduced through the courtesy of General Motors Corporation. Other photographs are by the author.

1 / *The Appeal of Antique Automobiles*

THE CARS START TO ASSEMBLE for the show early in the morning. A few of the very oldest arrive in trucks or aboard trailers, but most chug briskly on the field under their own power. There are black carriages on high wooden wheels that look as if they would be better off behind a horse; turn-of-the-century automobiles with upswept rear seats and sparkling brass radiators; splendid open-bodied touring cars of the Twenties and big boxy sedans of the Thirties — two-seaters, limousines, sports cars, station wagons, steamers, electric cars, even old-fashioned fire trucks, one of them complete with a barking Dalmatian dog.

All these fascinating vehicles park in long rows

across the still-wet grass; crowds of spectators begin to collect, and another antique car show is about to get under way. Such outdoor automotive exhibitions are becoming more and more popular in the United States for several reasons.

First of all, most Americans have loved cars since the days of those horseless carriages. And now that at least one motor vehicle exists for every two people in the United States and one of every seven jobs is in some way related to automobiles, more of the population than ever is car-minded.

But this constantly increasing number of automobiles has helped cause high accident rates,

Outdoor antique car shows are becoming increasingly popular in the United States.

traffic snarls and air pollution, not to mention a possible energy shortage. In contrast antique cars date from a happier time when we did not yet realize how serious these problems were going to be; and for this reason many people prefer old cars to current models.

An even more attractive feature of old cars is their individuality. Antique automobiles vary widely in construction, appearance and performance as compared to the standardized vehicles of today, all of which are pretty much alike. Usually designed by one man instead of by committees and computers like modern automobiles, antique cars are generally much more distinctive and have far greater character as a result.

Nearly everyone agrees about this strong appeal of old automobiles. Older spectators like to look at antique cars because they remember driving or riding in them when they were young. Younger viewers are interested to see earlier versions of what has become a central feature of their daily lives; and enthusiasts of all ages admire the skilled craftsmanship shown in the restoration of the cars to their exact original condition.

Some confusion does exist as to just which cars should be called "antique," though. While the public tends to apply the word generally to *all* old automobiles, the organizations of old-car owners are much more specific. The Antique Automobile Club of America, for instance, classifies only those cars built before 1930 as antique. You will see automobiles made between 1930 and 1950 at AACA meets, it is true: but they are officially called either "Production Cars" or "Classic Cars." The classification schemes of the many other old-car groups are apt to vary, and state requirements for "antique" license plates can be still different, thus making the term even more indefinite.

The fourteen antique cars described in the following three chapters were chosen to represent the first forty years of the American automobile, 1893 to 1932. Included are some of the most historically significant manufacturers, models and mechanical advances of that period. A few automobiles and incidents that are not so important appear as well, not only because they are amusing in themselves but also because they illustrate the engaging variety and individualism of nearly all old cars.

2 / *Automotive Pioneers*

Duryea. The automobile was not created at one specific point in history by a single individual but was developed gradually over a period of years by a number of inventors in several countries. After the work of earlier contributors has been recognized, credit for the first practical gasoline automobile is generally awarded to Karl Benz (1885) and Gottlieb Daimler (1886) of Germany.

Identifying the first successful gasoline automobile in the United States is also difficult because many men were tinkering on similar vehicles, all at just about the same time. Still, most historians now give the honor to the Duryea car of 1893 (photo).

Charles E. and J. Frank Duryea were brothers

who had come to Springfield, Massachusetts, because they were in the bicycle business, like so many of the other automotive pioneers. Charles, the elder, was a bicycle manufacturer back in Peoria, Illinois; and young Frank was an expert bicycle mechanic and toolmaker. While Charles was arranging to have his new "Sylph" bicycle made at a factory near Springfield, Frank worked there.

The two brothers were later to quarrel bitterly over which deserved more recognition for building their car, but it now seems clear that Charles thought of the idea and outlined it generally on paper in 1891. Frank then left his job and constructed the vehicle, working out most of the specific mechanical details as he went along.

The basis of the car was a second-hand carriage for ladies, bought by Charles for seventy dollars. The Duryeas then planned to add an engine, transmission and steering mechanism; but with Charles back in Peoria and giving advice by mail, Frank's progress was slow. For a time he was delayed by a bad case of typhoid fever, and he also ran into several serious mechanical problems.

Besides having to build a different type engine from that originally designed by Charles, Frank was forced to develop a new, electrical ignition system, devise a carburetor, and eventually invent a better

1893
Duryea

transmission for getting the engine's power to the wheels. Working until two A.M. morning after morning, he finally succeeded; and the car was able to travel about two hundred feet under its own power on September 21, 1893.

The one-cylinder, four-horsepower engine of

that first car was at its extreme rear, between the spindly forty-four-inch wheels. (The small tanks to be seen in the photograph above the engine are for gasoline and water.) Steering was done with a lever, called a tiller; and moving the tiller up and down also shifted gears.

An improved second Duryea, designed and built entirely by Frank, won the first automobile race to be held in the United States, fifty-five miles through snowy Chicago streets on Thanksgiving Day, 1895. Of six starters, only two finished; and the victorious Duryea averaged just over five miles an hour. The Duryea Motor Wagon Company had also been formed in 1895, and in 1896 it manufactured thirteen Duryeas for sale to the public. Charles and Frank were soon to disagree and pursue separate careers, but their short-lived company was the start of today's vast automotive industry.

Oldsmobile. Although some reports say the car was lost in a shipwreck, the first automobile to be exported from the United States was shipped to Bombay, India, in 1893. Built by Ransom Eli Olds of Lansing, Michigan, it was an improved version of a steam car that he had originally constructed six years earlier, when the Duryeas were still back in Peoria.

Olds was the son of a former blacksmith who

had given up shoeing horses for the more modern calling of operating a machine shop. Young Olds learned to be an expert machinist in his father's shop; and after he and his father had been making steam engines on a large scale for some time, they turned to the manufacture of gasoline engines.

Olds next attempted a gasoline-powered car, and, in common with other early automobile build-

1901
Oldsmobile

ers, found one of the biggest problems to be designing a workable gasoline engine that was small enough. Having completed the car in 1896, Olds then set up a company to make duplicates for sale; but he was much more successful than the Duryeas.

By 1901 the Olds Motor Works had developed no less than eleven different models, including some electric cars. That March, however, a raging fire swept through the factory, destroying everything. Everything that is except one small experimental runabout that a young worker was able to push out of the flames. The only survivor of the fire, it was immediately rushed into production.

Destined to become famous in a song—"Come Away With Me, Lucile, In My Merry Oldsmobile" —the light two-seater was much simpler and less expensive ($650) than the company's previous cars. With a wheelbase of only five and one-half feet and weighing but seven hundred pounds, the Merry Oldsmobile had a seven-horsepower, one-cylinder engine under its buggy-style seat. The thin wire-spoked wheels resembled those of a bicycle; the engine turned the rear axle by means of a chain; and there was no horn, a bicycle bell being standard equipment.

Steering was by tiller; and at its front the open carriage body swelled up into a graceful sleigh-like curve. For this reason this model is generally known as the curved-dash Oldsmobile. The photograph shows a 1901 car.

Ransom Olds was also a pioneer in automotive publicity; and tiny curved-dash Oldsmobiles were soon making demonstration climbs up the steps of many public buildings. They appeared at state fairs, too, where contests were often held to see how many people could be crammed aboard, seventeen thin passengers seeming to have been the record.

The biggest curved-dash promotional stunt of them all was Roy Chapin's trip from Detroit to New York City in 1901. Roy Chapin was a young photographer with the Olds Motor Works who was asked by Ransom Olds to drive a Merry Oldsmobile all the way to New York for the Second National Automobile Show in Madison Square Garden. The 820-mile journey, partly through Canada, was the longest ever made by motor car at the time; and it took seven and one-half days of difficult travel over narrow, rutted and twisting roads. Since it was fall, at least there was no mud; and Chapin also saved time by running along the straight path that paralleled the Erie Canal, ordinarily used only by the mules that towed barges along the waterway.

In spite of bending the front axle in Canada, having to rebuild the transmission in Peekskill,

New York, and skidding into a Fifth Avenue curb, Chapin rolled up to the Waldorf Astoria Hotel right on schedule. He was so dirty from repairing a wheel after the skid, however, that the doorman would not let him in the front door and Chapin had to go around to the back.

This famous trip sent the sales of curved-dash Oldsmobiles quickly upward; and the small runabout became the most popular car of its day, the first to be sold in relatively large quantities. Surprisingly enough, within a few years the Olds management decided to stop making the Merry Oldsmobile, turning to larger and more powerful cars instead. Ransom E. Olds, who disagreed, left both the organization and automobile bearing his name behind in 1904; from then until 1936 he manufactured a car carrying his initials, the Reo.

Stanley. During the early days of the automobile in this country, there was strong rivalry among gasoline-, electric- and steam-propelled cars. Gasoline-powered vehicles eventually proved more practical, of course; but in the beginning many experts thought steam cars would win out.

The Stanley steam car was probably the best, and it was certainly the only steamer to have been built by identical twins, so similar in appearance that even their employees could not tell them apart.

F.E. and F.O. Stanley were former country schoolteachers from Maine who had gone into business in Newton, Massachusetts, making photographic plates. At one time or another the bearded twins were also involved in the manufacture of violins, the invention of a home generator for lighting gas, and experimentation with early x-ray equipment.

1904
Stanley

Thus, when the versatile F.E. and F.O. saw a gasoline car from France break down during a demonstration run at the Brockton Fair, they decided to try building a car themselves. Their first "teakettle on wheels," finished in 1897, ran well; and after the twins had constructed two further-improved steamers, many people wanted to buy one. The Stanleys, always quick to know a good thing when they saw it, put their car into production in 1899.

When Stanley sales boomed, F.E. and F.O. showed themselves even shrewder businessmen by selling out for a quarter of a million dollars to individuals who ran things so poorly that the twins were soon able to buy their concern back for twenty thousand. They resumed making steamers in 1901 — a 1904 model is shown in the photograph — and continued until 1917 when both retired. The Stanley Motor Carriage Company then continued to produce cars, although at a steadily declining rate, until 1923.

Crusty individualists, the Stanleys sold only for cash, did not believe in advertising, and thought being asked to give a guarantee with one of their cars was an insult. As fast drivers themselves, they did regard racing as good publicity for a time, however. Special streamlined Stanleys, called "Wogglebugs," won many races; and Stanley cars were strong competitors during the annual winter "Speed Week" held on Ormond-Daytona Beach, Florida, in the early 1900's. Fred Marriott, head of the Stanley repair department, set a new World Land Speed Record of 127.66 mph there in 1906; but after his Bug crashed badly at 150 mph the following winter, the Stanleys gave up racing.

Stanley steamers were fast and smooth; very simple to drive and repair; and they were absolutely quiet. But Stanleys also required a long and complicated procedure of thirteen adjustments to get up steam before they could run; and many people unjustifiably feared a boiler explosion, too. In addition the handmade steam cars were much more expensive than mass-produced gasoline automobiles, so they gradually disappeared from the road.

Ford (Model T). Of all the five thousand makes and almost endless models of cars that have been built in this country and Canada, most important by far is the Model T Ford. Simple, tough and inexpensive, fifteen million Model T's were sold over a period of nineteen years; and they changed our way of life more than any other car.

In fact, Model T Fords became so well known all over the world that many people thought Henry Ford had invented the automobile. In reality his

1915
Ford Model T

first car, the "Quadricycle," was not completed until 1896, three years after the Duryea of 1893. Ford had made a rough sketch of the "Quadricycle" as early as 1891; but it was Christmas Eve, 1893, before he and his wife even tested his first gasoline engine in their kitchen sink.

Once the "Quadricycle" was running, Ford built two more experimental models and left his job as engineer for an electric lighting company to manufacture cars for sale. Not long afterward he also began building and driving racing cars for their publicity value; and at one point he held an unofficial World Land Speed Record of 91.37 mph.

Ford's first two attempts at manufacturing road cars were meanwhile both failures, but in 1903 his third try, the Ford Motor Company, was immediately successful. Among the original owners were the scrappy Dodge brothers, John and Horace, who gave up making transmissions for Oldsmobile to provide Ford with chassis, engines and transmissions built to Henry's designs. Except for bodies, wheels and a few other small parts, the Dodge brothers constructed all the Ford cars for the first three years, and a large proportion during the following seven. (In 1913 the Dodges were to leave Ford and start making their own automobiles. A much-told joke of the time claimed their cars needed no horns because they carried a warning on the front that read "Dodge Brothers.")

The first production Ford, a two-cylinder, Merry-Oldsmobile sort of car with its engine under the floor, was called Model A. In 1904 Model B, a much larger automobile with a four-cylinder engine, was also offered. Model C was an improved "A"; letters "D" and "E" were used for experimental models; and Model F, introduced in 1905, was a still-further-improved A. Sales of these cars were extremely good; and in 1906 the Ford Motor Company, then in only its fourth year, built more automobiles (8,729) than any other U.S. manufacturer.

A split had developed in its management, however, as reflected by Models K and N which came out late in 1905. Model K was a large and costly ($2,800) six-cylinder car, while Model N was a small, inexpensive ($500) four-cylinder vehicle; the argument was over whether to make luxury cars or automobiles for the average man. Henry Ford himself strongly favored the little N's, and when they sold much better than the big K's, the future course of the company was determined. R and S were built as fancy N's (1907), and next came the famous Model T.

The first Model T was made in 1908, the last in 1927; and during the intervening years millions of rattling, shaking flivvers poured out of the Ford factories to revolutionize daily living in the United States. For the first time a highly practical car was available that nearly everyone could afford, and as a result more and more Americans took to the road each year.

"Tin Lizzies" could run on any road in the

country, too, plus many places where there were no roads at all. The boxy Model T's were certainly no beauties; and with twenty-horsepower, four-cylinder engines they could only do forty miles an hour flat-out; but they were designed for rough use and were very sturdily built. In order to cover rough terrain their wheels were thirty inches in diameter and the springs were stiff; and Model T's were made of a special steel that was stronger and lighter than that used in other U.S. cars, even the most expensive. Called vanadium steel, it was first seen by Henry Ford when he examined the wreck of a French racing car on a Florida beach where he had brought a Model K to compete.

Besides being strong, T's were also very nimble, able to turn a circle in just a bit more than their length. They were also relatively easy to drive, the gears being shifted by means of foot pedals; and so simple to fix that an owner could do it himself. A farmer could even jack up his T, remove a rear wheel, belt his farm machinery to the rear axle and saw wood, grind grain or shear sheep.

With the price of a T getting down as low as $290 by 1924, there were no frills of any kind, not even a gas gauge; and the only way to tell how much gas was left was to stop, get out, unscrew the cap from the tank under the front seat, and put a stick inside. Since the gasoline was fed from the tank to the engine by gravity, it was often necessary to *back* up steep hills. And from 1914 until 1926, as Henry Ford himself said, you could have any color you liked, just as long as it was black. The reason was that black paint dried faster.

The T sold so well upon its introduction that the company quickly stopped making all the other model Fords to concentrate on increasing its production of T's. Even so, they could not be made fast enough to keep up with the great demand; and in 1913 Ford set up the first moving assembly line, reducing the time to build a car by more than one-half with this revolutionary manufacturing method. By 1915 there were over a million Model T's banging along U.S. roads, and from 1918 to 1925 they totaled more than one-half of all the cars in the country. The photograph is of a 1915 Model T.

3 / *Automobiles Become Big Business*

E.M.F. At the time Henry Ford decided to stop production of all other models and build only T's, not everyone thought he was making a wise move. One of those who disagreed was Walter E. Flanders, the Ford production manager who had developed the manufacturing procedures by which the Model T would be made.

Flanders left Ford in 1908, the year of the T's debut; and shortly afterwards he and two other automotive pioneers started the Everitt-Metzger-Flanders Company. B.F. Everitt was originally a carriage maker who had supplied upholstery for the curved-dash Oldsmobiles and who had also built the body for one of Henry Ford's first cars. "Smiling

Billy" Metzger was the former owner of a bicycle store who had become the first independent automobile dealer in the United States. In addition Metzger had been one of Henry Ford's early financial backers, a promoter of Detroit's first automobile race (won by Ford) and sales manager for Cadillac as well.

Although this trio also made a small twenty-horsepower "Flanders," their major car was the E.M.F. Thirty (photo), named for its horsepower. The E.M.F. had a wheelbase six inches longer than

E.M.F.

that of a Model T and cost $1,250. It was basically a sturdy enough automobile; but the gearbox was built as part of the rear axle, and this transmission-axle was subject to frequent failure. Consequently E.M.F. owners were always thinking up unflattering new names for their cars, ranging from "Every Man's Folly" to "Every Mechanical Fault"; with another favorite E.M.F. joke being to complain that the car needed service "Every Monday and Friday."

Everitt, Metzger and Flanders wanted an outside firm to handle the sales of their cars, for which they selected the Studebaker Brothers. Manufacturing Company of South Bend, Indiana. The five Studebakers were then the country's largest builder of horse-drawn vehicles, but they had recently started to make horseless carriages, too; and the cars of both firms were to be sold together.

This arrangement was barely underway when Flanders and the Studebaker company got into divisive business and legal arguments. Studebaker finally settled the whole thing by buying up "Every Mechanic's Friend"; and while E.M.F. had a very brief existence from 1909 until 1913 Studebakers were made until 1966.

Buick. Brought to this country from Scotland in 1856 when he was two years old, David D. Buick was left an orphan at the age of five. He grew up in Detroit, and as a teen-ager his first mechanical job was with the same machine shop that was also to give Henry Ford his start a few years later.

Buick eventually became a partner in a plumbing-supply business; and he invented a process by which the porcelain coating is applied to cast-iron bathroom fixtures, thereby creating the first modern bathtub. At the turn of the century he sold his valuable plumbing interests to concentrate on building gasoline engines in which he had grown much more interested.

Buick's first engines were intended for use on farms and in boats, but before long he decided to build engines for those newfangled horseless carriages, too. The next logical step was to construct the automobiles themselves; and Buick's cars turned out to be stronger, more reliable and quieter than others of the early 1900's, primarily because of his superior engines. Buick and two of his engineers had located the valves in the head right over the pistons, and these "valve-in-head" engines were much more powerful for their size. (The same overhead-valve principle is still used today in nearly all automobile engines.)

As good as Buick's experimental model was, he was a much better inventor than businessman; and

*1912
Buick*

he had great difficulties getting his car into production. At first, Benjamin and Frank Briscoe, sheet-metal manufacturers known for their garbage cans and having supplied bodies to Ransom Olds, gave him materials and money in exchange for financial control of his company. Then, in 1903, the Briscoes decided this was a bad investment and sold out to a man from Flint, Michigan, who moved the company there.

    The first twenty-seven production Buicks were

finally built in Flint during 1904, but by then the company was short of money again and had to be sold once more. This time control passed to a highly successful cart manufacturer and supersalesman, William C. Durant. He quickly made a great success of the organization at last; and by 1908 the Buick Motor Company was able to produce 8,820 cars, second only to Ford's 10,202.

Unlike Henry Ford who concentrated on one model at a time, Durant favored the modern practice of offering a wide variety of cars. In 1912, for instance, Buick buyers already had their choice of six models, including the sturdy touring car shown in the photograph.

Sad to say, David Buick had been squeezed out of the organization some time before. Tragically, the inventor Benjamin Briscoe once said had made a hundred other men millionaires was to have one business failure after another for the rest of his life and die in poverty. For that matter, hustling Billy Durant had also been toppled from power in Flint in 1910, but he was soon to regain leadership elsewhere in the rapidly expanding industry.

Maxwell. By July, 1894, less than a year after the Duryea made its first run in Massachusetts, a second successful internal combustion automobile had already been developed. Designed by Elwood

Haynes, a gas-company superintendent, the one-cylinder car was built in the Kokomo, Indiana, machine shop of the Apperson brothers.

One of the mechanics who worked on the car was Jonathan D. Maxwell, who later took a job at the Olds Motor Works where he became Chief Tester and worked on Roy Chapin's Detroit-to-New York car. Maxwell then left Olds to manufacture for a very short time a car that was at least partially of his own design, the "Silent Northern."

1911
Maxwell

During 1903 Maxwell also invented a system of engine cooling, the radiators for which were made by the Briscoe Manufacturing Company. Benjamin and Frank Briscoe had withdrawn their financial support from David Buick that same year; and when Maxwell designed a new car, Benjamin Briscoe went into partnership with him for its manufacture in Tarrytown, New York.

The first Maxwell-Briscoes, produced in 1904, were either a light two-passenger roadster with an eight-horsepower, two-cylinder engine that sold for $700; or a larger four-passenger touring car of fourteen horsepower costing $1550. As with several other early automobiles the handbrake of these Maxwells was connected to the clutch, so it was not necessary to use the clutch pedal when starting. Once the tiny engine was popping, easing off on the hand-brake alone would put the car in motion; and the clutch pedal was not needed until it was time to change gears.

The year after the Maxwell-Briscoe was introduced, Jonathan Maxwell drove a roadster and Benjamin Briscoe a touring car in the first Glidden Tour. Sponsored by Charles J. Glidden, a retired millionaire, the Glidden Tours were annual endurance runs held between 1905 and 1913 to demonstrate the reliability and convenience of the automobile as a new means of transportation. The demanding 870-mile route in 1905 started in New York City and wound through New England, including two difficult climbs of Mount Washington in New Hampshire.

A Pierce-Arrow won that first Glidden Tour; and Maxwell and Pierce, usually the lowest- and highest-priced cars on the tour, were to become bitter rivals throughout the remainder of the series. In 1911, the year of the Maxwell roadster in the photograph, a factory team of three Maxwells won the Glidden Trophy on a lengthy Tour from New York to Jacksonville, Florida.

The Maxwell company's best sales performance relatively speaking was in 1909 when it ranked right behind Ford and Buick. Jonathan Maxwell left in 1912 during a financial reorganization, with Walter Flanders coming in as head of the new management. (It had also been Flanders' E.M.F. group that had absorbed the company making Maxwell's "Silent Northern" in 1908.)

Faltering Maxwell fortunes made a second reorganization necessary in 1921; and former president of Buick Walter P. Chrysler was next to take over. Within a few years he was able to transform the company into the nucleus of today's powerful Chrysler Corporation, the little Maxwell first becoming a Chrysler and then being turned into the Plymouth in 1928.

Brush. Part of the time that his older brother Benjamin was involved with the Maxwell, Frank Briscoe was president of his own automobile manufacturing organization, the Brush Runabout Company. Named for its designer, Alanson P. Brush, the little Brush Runabout was even lower-priced ($485) than the Maxwell.

Brush had helped design the first Cadillac as well as the engine of the Oakland, a forerunner of the Pontiac; but he wanted the automobile named after him to be smaller and less costly. Like the curved-dash Oldsmobile and the Model T (Brush had gone to school with Henry Ford), the Brush Runabout was intended to be a simple and inexpensive car for the average family, costing less to buy and operate than a horse and buggy.

Only seven feet long and less than five feet wide, the Brush had a small one-cylinder, ten-horsepower engine that allowed the car a top speed of thirty miles an hour. The rear wheels were turned by chains, much like a bicycle, making Brushes good climbers; and a big lever located outside the body was used to shift gears.

While the Brush was thus quite similar to other cars of the period in many respects, it was markedly

1907
Brush

different in others. It was one of the first cars to have a fuel pump instead of depending on gravity to get gasoline into the engine, for instance. The Brush was also one of the first cars in the United States to have its driver located on the left side instead of on the right side as was done in Europe, thus making it easier for Americans to see ahead as they drove on the right side of the road. And, in addition, the

Brush was one of the first automobiles in this country to have a coil-spring suspension.

Most unusual of all about the Brush, though, was the fact that it was made chiefly of wood for both lightness and low cost. Nearly all cars of that period had wooden wheels; but the body, frame and even the axles of the Brush were also wooden. The standard joke for the Brush owners was therefore that their car had a "wooden body, wooden axles, wooden wheels . . . and wooden run."

In spite of the joke, Brushes ran well enough as compared to other cars of the day; and in 1910 a little red Brush Runabout was used for a long test drive from New York City to Cross Roads, Oklahoma, by Bud and Temple Abernathy. Since Temple and Bud were ten and six years old at the time and had already ridden alone from Oklahoma to New York on horseback to meet their father, their trip was all the more incredible. Mr. Abernathy did not know how to drive, so he followed along behind the boys in a chauffeur-driven Maxwell.

Although advertised as "Everyman's Car," the Brush Runabout never really sold that well and was to have a brief life in the bargain. The first Brushes were made in 1907 (photo) and three years later the Brush organization became part of the ill-fated United States Motor Company. This was a large

General Motors-type combination of 130 companies headed by Benjamin Briscoe, with Maxwell-Briscoe as its base. Greatly overexpanded, the United States Motor Company went bankrupt in 1912, and only the Maxwell survived.

Briscoe. After the collapse of the United States Motor Company an undaunted Benjamin Briscoe went to France, where he set up Briscoe Frères to manufacture small cars. But by 1914 he had returned to this country to found the Briscoe Motor Company with money provided by the Swifts, a wealthy meat-packing family from Chicago.

Frank also had an interest in the Briscoe Motor Company, as had been true of most of Benjamin's other projects including financial help to Charles Duryea in 1907. This time the car, built in Jackson, Michigan, was named the "Briscoe"; and because Benjamin had brought its design back with him from France, he liked to call it "The First French Car at an American Price."

The Briscoe was a small car weighing only 1700 pounds, with a four-cylinder, twenty-four-horsepower engine in the first versions and a V-8 engine available in later years. The first models sold for $750, and in a signed advertisement Benjamin Briscoe explained that this price was very low because "we are satisfied with small profit" and "are not desirous of getting rich too rapidly." Possibly this was true, but the price was also low because it did not include the top, windshield, starter and generator, all of which were extras! An equipped Briscoe cost $900 initially, although it must be added that this price did come down in time and that other manufacturers also used similar pricing practices.

While not a particularly striking car in any other way, a Briscoe was instantly recognizable by its

1915
Briscoe

single headlight mounted at the top of the radiator. Bystanders never failed to take a second look when they spotted the "Cyclops Eye"; and as the photograph of a 1915 Briscoe touring car shows, many spectators at antique car meets still do so today.

Briscoe cars did not sell as well as those which the brothers had made under other people's names; and the Briscoe Motor Company had to stop production in 1922. Essentially the same automobile was then made as the Earl by another company for two more years.

Another irony of the Briscoe story is that Benjamin had brought plans for a very small motorcycle-type car back from France along with those for the bigger Briscoe; and he had also organized the Argo Motor Company in Jackson to manufacture this cyclecar. After only two years the unsuccessful Argo cyclecar became known as the Hackett; and three years later its manufacture was taken over by the Lorraine Motors Corporation of Grand Rapids. The Lorraine Motors Corporation existed for only two years before it, too, failed; and owning controlling interest at the time was David Buick.

4 / *The Automobile Age Arrives*

Chevrolet. Bushy-mustached Louis Chevrolet was one of three Swiss brothers, all racing drivers, who came to this country from France. In 1908 he and brother Arthur joined the factory racing team then being assembled by William Durant, who had recently taken control of Buick. The Buick racing team, formed by Durant to test engines as well as create publicity, won many races, traveling as far as Europe to compete.

Meanwhile, Durant was engaging in some competition of his own inside the executive offices. Using Buick as his base and later buying the Olds Motor Works, in 1908 he founded the General Motors Company which would eventually become the largest business enterprise in the world.

1918
Chevrolet

Durant's next move was to acquire more than twenty other companies for General Motors, including Cadillac and Oakland (now Pontiac), plus the rights to Frenchman Albert Champion's sparkplugs. Even Henry Ford hinted that he might sell to the aggressive Durant at this point; but the deal fell through when Ford specified that his eight-million-dollar price be paid in cash, something Durant was finding increasingly difficult to raise just then.

Part of Durant's trouble was caused by the many weak companies he had purchased; and successful as the Buick operation was, it could not make up for all these losses. By late 1910 General Motors had to borrow fifteen million dollars; and the lending bankers insisted that as one of the conditions for their loan Durant be removed from power.

Within a year Durant was back in action, however. In 1911 he formed the Mason Motor Company in Flint (Mason had formerly built Buick engines); the Little Motor Car Company in Flint (named after the ex-Buick general manager, not the size of its cars); and the Chevrolet Motor Company in Detroit. By then Louis Chevrolet had become a very famous racing driver; and in return for ownership of much of the company, he not only allowed the use of his name, he also designed—with some help—the first model of the Chevrolet.

A large, powerful and expensive six-cylinder automobile that cost $2,150, Chevrolet's design did not sell as well as the smaller $650 four-cylinder Littles. In 1913 Durant therefore combined the two companies for greater efficiency which so insulted Louis Chevrolet that he promptly left the organization and sold Durant all the stock that would have made him a very rich man. (Chevrolet was later to design the "American" automobile, a failure in spite of its cheery slogan, "America's Smile Car.")

The Chevrolet company then concentrated

more and more on building low-priced automobiles, the 490 Chevvie of 1915 being named after its eventual price. In 1917 Chevrolet built 110,839 cars; and as its production increased dramatically over the next ten years, it edged closer and closer to Ford for the national sales leadership. (A Chevrolet of 1918 is shown in the photograph.)

Finally, in 1927 when 1,749,998 Chevrolets were produced, Chevrolet became the best-selling car in the United States for the first time. The switch to a six-cylinder engine (nicknamed the "Cast Iron Wonder" and the "Stove-Bolt Six") was made in 1929; and from 1931 on Chevrolet has outsold all other U.S. cars in nearly every year.

This great advance by Chevrolet enabled William Durant to quietly trade Chevrolet stock for shares of General Motors; and by a 1915 GM Board of Directors' meeting he owned enough GM stock to walk in and announce that he controlled the company, completely flabbergasting the financial world. In 1916 Durant was therefore able to return as the central figure of General Motors for the second time.

Chevrolet was made a division of General Motors in 1918; and Durant stayed as overall head of the organization for the next two years. During the depression of 1920, however, he was again forced out of General Motors as part of still another major financial reorganization. Although he was to have a short period of success with Durant Motors after that, he was later reduced to declaring personal bankruptcy. Like David Buick, Durant died in obscurity.

Hudson. Three years after his historic drive from Detroit to the 1901 New York automobile show, Roy D. Chapin became the Olds Motor Works' first sales manager. Wanting to go into business for himself, he next left Olds in 1906 and got financial backing from E.R. Thomas. (Thomas automobiles were made in Buffalo, New York; and a Thomas Flyer was to win the astounding New York-to-Paris race of 1908, twenty-two thousand miles long and nearly around the world.)

Chapin was later joined by several other former Olds executives, including the man who had rescued the curved-dash Oldsmobile from the fire; and Howard Coffin, the very talented chief engineer at Olds. This group then formed a company to make automobiles designed by Coffin and sold to the public by Thomas.

In 1909, when Coffin had come up with a much-improved model, Chapin, Coffin and two other ex-Olds employees split off to set up still another organization. This time they received most of their money from J.L. Hudson, uncle of the wife of one member of the group and owner of Detroit's biggest department store; and the new car was called the Hudson. After all, as more than one writer has pointed out, they could hardly follow the usual custom of naming the car for its designer.

Hudsons quickly established themselves as solid, well-built cars; and over the years the Hudson Motor Car Company was responsible for several technical advances. One of these was an engine crankshaft that was weighted to be in perfect bal-

1923
Hudson

ance as it was spun around by the rods from the sliding pistons. First used in the 1916 Super-Six, this crankshaft not only smoothed out the usual violent engine shake of the time, it also permitted much higher crankshaft speeds, thereby producing more power from the same size engine.

The Hudson was first made as a low-priced four-cylinder car, then gradually became a medium-priced six-cylinder automobile of which the 1923 model in the photograph is an example. To broaden the line Chapin introduced the low-priced four-cylinder Essex (later called the Terraplane) in 1919; and the Essex soon became a strong rival of the Model T's.

Already more than twice as powerful as the T, the Essex gained another advantage in 1921. Until then the few totally enclosed "all-weather" cars were very expensive, the majority of automobiles having open bodies (photo) with folding cloth tops, and side curtains that could be buttoned on in case of cold or rain. As a result many people did not drive cars on bad days or in severe climates. By putting flat metal sheets over a box-shaped wooden frame, however, the builders of the Essex were able to give it a closed body costing only $300 more than the touring version.

After the Hudson had also received a similar

body, Chapin worked hard to bring the prices of his closed cars even lower; and by 1925 an Essex sedan cost only $895, which was five dollars *less* than an Essex tourer. This caused the other manufacturers to concentrate on building the more practical sedans too, a move that was to make automobiles sell even faster in the long run.

Chapin died in 1936, and by then the other "Olds alumni" had either died or retired, too. Only fifteen years remained for Hudson automobiles (no civilian cars were made for three years during World War II); and in 1954 the Hudson Motor Car Company had to be merged with another floundering automobile manufacturer, Nash, to form the present American Motors Corporation.

Cadillac. When Ransom Olds put the curved-dash Oldsmobile into production after the fire he needed engines in a hurry, so he placed orders with both the Dodge brothers and stern Henry M. Leland, who ran the best machine shop in Detroit. While each part of the Oldsmobile engine was required to measure within one one-hundredth of an inch of its specified size, this represented no problem at all to the demanding Leland because he was accustomed to allowing tolerances of only one-thousandth.

After Leland's shop had been turning out Oldsmobile engines for a time, his engineers made a special version that had several improvements and was built to one-thousandth-of-an-inch tolerances. This new engine was more than twice as powerful, but the Olds management decided to continue using the less precisely made original, probably for reasons of cost.

Shortly afterwards Leland was asked to appraise the machinery of the Henry Ford Company. This was the second of Henry Ford's two false starts before the success of the Ford Motor Company; Henry himself had just left and the company was about to go out of business. Instead of setting a value on the machinery, however, Leland recommended that the company stay in operation, using his Oldsmobile-type engine in its cars.

As a result the Henry Ford Company was reorganized in 1902 as the Cadillac Automobile Company, named for the French explorer who founded Detroit. The first Cadillacs, made in Leland's machine shop, were small, one-cylinder cars costing only $850; and they became very popular, outselling all other makes except Oldsmobile from 1904 until 1906. Nevertheless, Henry Leland and his son Wilfred had taken over management of Cadillac in 1904, and they were to gradually develop models of increasing quality and price.

Rather than continue making each part fit only one car as was generally done at the time, Henry Leland was one of the first to see the importance of building cars with standard interchangeable parts. As a demonstration of this idea in England in 1908, three Model K Cadillacs were taken apart, some parts changed for spares, all the parts scrambled and then assembled again. Each of the three cars ran perfectly for five hundred miles, and Cadillac was awarded the Dewar Trophy for the accomplishment.

A second Dewar Trophy was given Cadillac in 1913 for its electric self-starter and lighting system. Cadillac's starter was the first practical device of its kind, finally ending the nuisance and danger of hand-cranking cars to start them. Since the Cadillac needed a large battery to supply power for its starter anyway, the Lelands' engineers took advantage of it to also provide the car with electric lights. These two advances, soon adopted by other car makers as well, added greatly to the general use of automobiles.

Henry and Wilfred Leland left Cadillac in 1917 to later build another luxury car, named after Henry's idol, Abraham Lincoln. By then Cadillac had been owned by William Durant's General Motors for eight years; and as part of that giant cor-

*1924
Cadillac*

poration it has continued making prestigious vehicles until the present. The photograph shows a 1924 model.

Packard. The first of two traditional Packard stories is an explanation of why James W. Packard built his own automobile in the first place. This anecdote relates that in 1898 Packard bought Alexander Winton's twelfth car (Wintons were made in Cleveland, Ohio, from 1897 until 1924), that the car broke down time after time, and that Packard complained angrily to Winton. An insulted Winton is then supposed to have snapped something like "If you think you can do better, try it," whereupon

Packard is said to have replied, with much determination, "I will!"

In reality it is likely that James Packard and his brother William had already been thinking about building a car long before this happened. Whatever the circumstances, they did hire two men away from Winton and started constructing an automobile in a corner of the Warren, Ohio, factory where they made electrical supplies. The Model A Packard, a one-cylinder runabout first called an "Ohio," was completed in 1899; and it was such a good automobile that James Packard decided to put it on the market.

According to the second favorite Packard story, it was about this time that the famous slogan originated. A letter is reported to have arrived at the factory asking for a sales pamphlet describing the car; and because none was yet available, James Packard is quoted as instructing, "Tell them to . . . 'Ask the Man Who Owns One.' "

By 1901 the Model C Packard already had a steering wheel in place of a tiller, the first car to do so. The 1901 Packard was the first automobile to have its gearshift lever move in the now-familiar "H" pattern, too. But unfortunately for James Packard, 1901 was also the year in which he began to lose control of the company he had started.

Henry B. Joy, the son of a founder of the Chicago, Burlington and Quincy Railroad, had gone to the New York automobile show that fall to buy a car. (This was the same show to which Roy Chapin had driven the Oldsmobile.) Joy quickly decided against a steamer that was displayed there after it had showered him with hot water; but when he saw a man start a Model C Packard at the curb with a single twirl of the crank to chase a horse-driven fire engine, he bought one like it.

Back home and well satisfied with his Packard, Joy invested heavily in the company and soon came to dominate its management. He moved the Packard organization to Detroit in 1903, eventually taking over as president from James Packard, who chose to remain in Warren.

The first car to be driven across the United States was a secondhand two-cylinder, twenty-horsepower Winton owned by a doctor from Vermont. To collect a fifty-dollar bet, he left San Francisco in late May, 1903, and arrived in New York City sixty-four days later. The second automobile to complete the adventurous four-thousand-mile journey was a much smaller one-cylinder, twelve-horsepower Model F Packard called "Old Pacific." Driven by a Packard shop foreman and an early automotive writer, "Old Pacific" left San Francisco four weeks after "The Vermont" and beat the larger Winton's record by three days.

In 1915 the public was so astonished by the new Twin-six Packard, which had a twelve-cylinder, eighty-five horsepower engine with the first aluminum pistons, that showrooms had to stay open all night. Later a racing car was built with a modified version of this engine; and in 1919 on Ormond-Daytona Beach it set a new U.S. Land Speed Record of 149.875 mph.

Like Cadillac, the Packard company became prosperous during the Twenties and early Thirties

1931
Packard

by building long, luxurious and expensive cars. (The eight-cylinder 1931 model in the photograph has a second windshield to protect passengers in the rear seat when the top is down.) But both the quality and sales of Packards declined sharply after World War II, and the once-great make slowly collapsed during the mid-Fifties.

Ford (Model A). By 1927 even Henry Ford himself had to agree that his elderly Model T was out of date. Other low-priced cars had become more powerful and were more comfortable, included such recent improvements as self-starters in their standard equipment, and also came in more colors. Sales of T's were falling off badly, which meant that a new model was needed as soon as possible.

Unlike today, when a new model is developed at the same time an old one is still being made, the Ford factory simply shut down in late May of 1927 and did not start production again until that October. An entirely new Ford was designed, its prodection methods worked out, and the machinery needed to make the car devised during that relatively short interval.

All this was done in the deepest secrecy as curiosity steadily increased throughout the United States. Some said the new Ford would have six cylinders, some thought it would be a V-8, and still others were absolutely certain that it would be named "Edison" after the inventor who was a close friend of Henry Ford's. Without even knowing its price, 500,000 people placed deposits on the car, whatever it turned out to be; and as a news story that year the coming of the new Ford ranked second only to Lindbergh's trans-Atlantic flight.

With suspense heightening all the more, the much-awaited new models finally began to arrive at dealers' showrooms covered with canvas so they still could not be seen. Then, when they were displayed at last, the milling crowds grew so large in several cities that police had to be called in to restore order.

What the excited viewers saw were cars like the snappy little roadster in the photograph. Except for having the same springs, the same number of cylinders (four) and a similar low starting price ($385), they were nothing at all like the Model T. Perhaps to show just how new they were, the Ford company had gone all the way back to the beginning of the alphabet again and called them "Model A."

The Model A was almost a foot lower and two feet longer than a Model T with much more up-to-date styling. Its forty-horsepower engine gave the A a top speed of sixty miles an hour, and for the first time a Ford had four-wheel brakes. There was a standard three-speed transmission that was shifted by hand instead of with foot pedals like the T; and the A's accelerator was worked by foot instead of by hand. The Model A Ford was also the first low-priced car to have a safety-glass windshield; and just in front of the windshield was the cap of the gas-tank by which any Model A can be easily spotted.

Nearly five million A's of only slightly differing specifications were made during the model's four-year history; but in 1932 the Model A had to be dropped in favor of still newer V-8 models to keep

Ford Model A

up with the fast-selling Chevrolet sixes. The end of the Model A thus marked the beginning of the modern automobile age; from then on an annual model change, even if only a slight change of appearance, became common as competition intensified. The fifty-millionth U.S. motor vehicle had already been made the year before; and if that was not enough of a signal that the automobile was revolutionizing American life, the year after the Model A was withdrawn from production, the first drive-in movie in the country opened.

5 / Seeing Antique Cars

A GOOD WAY TO GET A close-up look at cars like those in the preceding chapters is to visit a museum. The "first," very-oldest or only-known specimens are apt to be found in the transportation sections of large general museums or local historical collections. For instance, the Smithsonian Institution of Washington, D.C., exhibits the 1893 Duryea, the 1894 Haynes, the last remaining Olds of 1897 and the 1903 coast-to-coast Winton.

As you might expect, the Henry Ford Museum in Dearborn, Michigan, has many early Fords, including the 1896 "Quadricycle"; but a large number of other makes, such as an 1896 Duryea and the "Old Pacific" Packard, can also be seen there. And, as one further example, the Sloan Museum of Flint,

Michigan, contains William Durant's first cart, a 1910 Buick from his racing team and the very first Chevrolet.

In addition to these, there is also a much larger group of specialized museums devoted exclusively to old cars. While these museums may have a small number of very early or rare vehicles on display, too, their basic objective is to show representative examples of the many production automobiles of the past. Most inclusive by far is Harrah's Automobile Collection in Reno, Nevada, which now

"Get close, but please don't touch!"

totals more than 1,400 cars; but there are may other excellent collections in all parts of the coutry. A list of some of the major automotive collections and museums in the United States and Canada is the final chapter of this book.

In many respects, attending an antique car show can be even more fun. They are ordinarily held out of doors, are often accompanied by oldtime music, and usually have snack tents like a carnival. At an outdoor meet spectators not only see a wide variety of vehicles at rest, they can watch — and hear — them in motion. There can also be opportunities to talk with the owners of the cars and ask them questions; once in a while there may even be a chance to ride in an antique car.

(While it is possible to get close enough to the cars at an outdoor meet to touch them, please don't. Rare to begin with, antique cars have been painstakingly rebuilt and are therefore of great value. Then, too, the owner is likely to have been up very late the night before the show polishing all that brass; he won't like fingerprints, even admiring ones.)

At most meets the cars are judged for the accuracy of their restoration within categories, prizes being awarded at the end of the day. The detailed examination of the judges as they hover over and

An antique automobile horn goes up for auction.

under each car interests many spectators; and a crowd also collect when the performance tests are held. These include such events as attempts to balance a car at the center of a giant seesaw in the fastest time, races to see who can get his or her crank-type car started first, and speed competitions among the owners of touring cars at putting up their complicated tops.

Another typical feature of most antique car

meets is the flea market where old automobile parts are swapped and sold. The hobby of restoring old cars has now become so popular that some replacement parts are being made again; but the original items are usually preferred, despite surface rust and grease. They can be quite hard to find, of course; so flea-market searchers can occasionally be seen with "Wanted" signs on their backs or in their hats listing parts they currently need but have not been able to locate.

Unless you know someone who has an antique car, or wait until you see several well-shined beauties spinning along the highway early on a weekend morning and follow them, it may be difficult to learn just when an antique car show is to be held in your area. Public libraries should be able to help here, particularly if they subscribe to either "Old Cars" or "Hemmings Motor News."

These publications also list when and where the less-common antique car auctions take place. You might like to attend one of these, too, and see how some enthusiasts buy and sell both parts and entire cars. If a 1929 Model J Duesenberg comes on the block while you are there, don't nod at the auctioneer, though. The last one to be sold brought two hundred and seven thousand dollars.

6 / *Antique Car Museums*

ARKANSAS	The Museum of Automobiles	Route 3, Morrilton
CALIFORNIA	Briggs Cunningham Automotive Museum	250 E. Baker St., Costa Mesa
	Los Angeles County Museum of Natural History	900 Exposition Boulevard, Los Angeles
	Movieworld Cars of the Stars	6920 Orangethorpe Ave., Buena Park
COLORADO	Forney Transportation Museum	1416 Platte Street, Denver
DISTRICT OF COLUMBIA	Smithsonian Institution, Museum of History and Technology, Vehicle Hall	Constitution Ave. at 14th St.
FLORIDA	Bellm Cars of Yesterday	5500 North Tamiami Trail, Sarasota
	Early American Museum	Route 40, Silver Springs
	Elliott Museum of Vehicular Evolution	Route 5, Stuart
GEORGIA	Antique Auto and Music Museum	2542 Young Road, Stone Mountain
ILLINOIS	Chicago Historical Antique Automobile Museum	3160 Skokie Valley Road, Highland Park
	Museum of Science and Industry	Jackson Park, Chicago

/ 61

KANSAS	Billue's Antique Car Museum	Route 81, Hesston
MASSACHUSETTS	Heritage Plantation of Sandwich	Grove and Pine Sts., Sandwich
	Museum of Transportation	15 Newton St., Brookline
	Sturbridge Auto Museum	Route 20, Sturbridge
MICHIGAN	Detroit Historical Museum	5401 Woodward Ave., Detroit
	Greenfield Village and Henry Ford Museum	Oakwood Blvd., Dearborn
	Poll Museum	353 East 6th St., Holland
	Sloan Museum	303 Walnut St., Flint
MINNESOTA	Hemp Museum	Country Club Road, Rochester
MISSOURI	Autos of Yesteryear	Route 63, Rolla
	Kelsey's Antique Cars	Route 564, Camdenton
NEBRASKA	Harold Warp Pioneer Village	Routes 6 and 34, Minden
NEVADA	Harrah's Automobile Collection	East 2nd St., Reno
NEW JERSEY	Roaring 20 Autos	Route 34 and Ridgewood Rd., Wall
NEW YORK	Long Island Automotive Museum	Route 27, Southhampton
	Upstate Auto Museum	Route 20, Bridgewater
OHIO	Crawford Auto-Aviation Museum	10825 East Blvd., Cleveland
OKLAHOMA	Horseless Carriages Unlimited	2215 West Shawnee St., Muskogee
PENNSYLVANIA	Automobilorama	Route 15, Harrisburg
	Boyertown Museum of Historic Vehicles	Warwick St., Boyertown
	Pollock Auto Showcase	Route 30, Downingtown
	Swigart Museum	Route 22, Huntingdon
SOUTH DAKOTA	Horseless Carriage Museum	Route 16, Rapid City
VIRGINIA	Roaring Twenties Antique Car Museum	Route 230, Hood
ALBERTA, CANADA	Reynolds Museum	Highway 2A, Wetaskiwin
SASKATCHEWAN, CANADA	Western Development Museum	2610 Lorne Ave. S., Saskatoon

II
STEAM CARS

Acknowledgments

A number of steam enthusiasts have aided in the preparation of this book, but particular thanks are owed Frank H. Gardner, President of the Antique Auto Museum at Larz Anderson Park, Brookline, Massachusetts, for his generous cooperation. And, as always, James J. Bradley, Head of the Automotive History Collection of the Detroit Public Library, has been more than helpful in locating photographs.

The photographs on pages 74, 85, 87, 94, 95, 97 and 101 are reproduced from the Automotive History Collection, Detroit Public Library. Those on pages 66 and 98 were supplied by Brown Brothers, New York.

1 / F. E. and F. O.

NOT MANY PEOPLE in Newton, Massachusetts, in 1897 had seen an automobile before. Fewer still had seen anything like the unusual vehicle that suddenly appeared on the city's streets one day in September. Mounted on bicycle wheels but otherwise looking much like a carriage without a horse, the strange car rolled quietly along, puffing white clouds of steam and whistling softly like a kettle on a hot stove.

The two men in the open automobile attracted almost as much attention as their car. They were identical twins, dressed exactly alike in long black overcoats and black derby hats. Both had bushy black beards, and, as their car hissed toward Newtonville Square, the pair stared ahead with similar watchful expressions.

F. E. and F. O. Stanley in their first car.

They were F. E. and F. O. Stanley, testing the first of their many famous steam cars. The "teakettle on wheels" had already frightened one horse so badly that he had run away from his wagon, and the twins were proceeding cautiously. They were also keeping a close eye on their steam-pressure gauge, for pressure that was too low would not move the car, and pressure that was too high might cause a boiler explosion.

The Stanley twins were able to complete that first run without breaking down or exploding, and they made a longer trip to Cambridge the following day. Another skitterish horse bolted from his carriage as soon as he saw the car; but the steamer ran steadily again, and the brothers considered their first automobile to have proven itself.

These were the pioneer days of the motorcar in America, and men like the Stanleys were building self-propelled vehicles all over the country. Some were constructing cars operated by electric batteries; others were experimenting with gasoline engines; and many, like the Stanleys, were using steam as power.

The rivalry among electricity, gasoline and steam was to continue for several years before gasoline eventually became the established method of propelling automobiles. But at the time the Stanleys were working on their first car, many experts regarded steam as the most likely possibility.

Steam was used to power the first self-propelled vehicle that has been authenticated, a tractor built in Paris in 1769 by Nicolas Cugnot. The first vehicle in the United States capable of moving itself was also driven by steam: in 1805 Oliver Evans put wheels under his new steam dredge and used the steam engine to move the dredge down to the river where it was to work. By the 1820's and 1830's, steam-powered stage coaches were running on scheduled routes in England, while Sylvester H. Roper built several "road locomotives" in Massachusetts during the 1860's.

The reason most Americans were steam-minded at the turn of the century, however, was the recent and rapid growth of railroads in this country. The Civil War had stimulated much railroad construction; the first transcontinental railroad had been completed in 1869, and long trains pulled by steam locomotives chuffed in and out of most U. S. cities. Steam had become the most familiar form of mechanical power in the United States, and its long usage had provided much technical knowledge that would be helpful in automotive applications.

On the other hand, the gasoline engine was a relatively recent invention that had been used to power vehicles for only a short time. The first successful gasoline automobile was that of Karl Benz, built in Germany in 1885, more than a hundred years after Cugnot. Charles and Frank Duryea of Springfield, Massachusetts, at the opposite end of the state from F. E. and F. O., had built the first gasoline car in the United States in 1893, only four years before the Stanley. Most people were not yet accustomed to riding "over an explosion," as one manufacturer put it.

And those newfangled electric motors were just as mysterious as gasoline engines to the average man, not to mention that electric cars needed frequent charging of their batteries, which limited them to short trips around town. All things considered, steam seemed the power of the future to many early automobile enthusiasts.

Not that the Stanleys had previously been steam men—or automotive men of any kind, for that matter. F. E. (Francis Edgar) and F. O. (Freelan Oscar) were born on a farm in Kingfield, Maine, in 1849, and were country schoolteachers as young men. F. E., who also drew crayon portraits in his spare time, gave up teaching when he was twenty-five to become a full-time portrait artist in Lewiston, Maine.

While there, he became greatly interested in photography and was soon known as one of the best portrait photographers in New England. In those days, photography was a difficult and often messy process. Roll film had not yet been invented, photographers taking their pictures on sheets of glass coated with a chemical sensitive to light. The coating was applied to the glass plates in a solution of alcohol, ether and guncotton; and the plates had to be exposed and developed while they were still wet.

After F.E. had put up with these clumsy wet plates for a time, he invented a dry plate that was much more convenient to use. His new plates worked so well that he decided to manufacture them for other photographers, going into partnership with F.O., who had also left teaching and had been making mechanical-drawing sets until his factory burned down. Stanley photographic plates were shortly being sold all over the world, and the demand became so great that a larger factory was needed. In 1890, the brothers opened a new plant in Newton, Massachusetts, where railroad connections were better than in Lewiston.

The two Stanleys were independent men with strong opinions, and they ran their plate company and automobile business that followed to suit themselves and no one else. They purposely kept their organizations small so they could be inventors, executives, foremen, salesmen and stockholders all at the same time; and they were later reported as refusing to sell cars to would-be buyers whom they believed unworthy of owning a Stanley. They were convinced that good products needed no paid advertising, and they were against installment buying, selling only for cash. And they refused to give written guarantees, believing customers should be able to trust them without such documents.

Their employees have said that no matter what time they came to work in the morning, they always found the twins there first, sitting on either side of the front door, whittling and talking over their plans for the day. F.E. and F.O. looked so much alike that the workers could not tell them apart; and because the interchangeable brothers alternated in their office and plant duties, the men were always uncertain as to which was which. Not only did the two Stanleys look exactly alike, they also had similar signatures, and the Patent Office thought the same man had signed both names to their dry-plate patent application.

A mechanic named Fred Marriott, who later became a famous driver of racing Stanleys, finally discovered a method of identifying the twins—or so he later said to a writer, anyway. Marriott would tell a joke to F.E. and F.O. at the same time and wait for their reaction. According to Marriott's story, the twin who slapped his leg and said "Godfrey mighty!" was F.E., and the twin who slapped his leg and said "Gee cracky!" was F.O.

F.E. and F.O. always had a wide range of interests beyond their immediate concern. As a sideline, they once invented and manufactured a home generator of lighting gas, and for a time they experimented with early-day X-ray equipment as well. Both were excellent mathematicians and self-taught violin makers, and, like so many other inventors of the time, they were also very curious about automobiles.

F.E. had seen a steam car in Lewiston as early as 1887, but it was a crude affair that spouted thick black smoke and snapping sparks, almost hitting a telegraph pole during its test run. It has also been reported that the brothers saw a steam car in Boston in 1896 and bought some of the engineering details from its inventor, a Mr. Wagner. That fall F.E. and F.O. went to the Brockton Fair to see a De Dion Bouton gasoline car that had been imported from France. After examining the De Dion closely and watching it break down during a demonstration run, the twins told each other they could probably do better themselves.

The Stanleys went home, thought it over, and decided to build a car of their own. After settling on steam as their source of power, they ordered a small steam engine, had a suitable boiler built, and bought a light buggy from a carriage shop. When they began to assemble these parts, they discovered that the engine and boiler together weighed over six hundred pounds, causing the finished automobile to be slow and awkward.

Unwieldy as it was, the car astounded the residents (and horses) of Newton by running under its own power on two successive trips. Pleased with this result, the two brothers immediately started on three improved models: a two-seater for F.E., a two-seater for F.O., and a four-seater that was never completed. This time they designed and built their own explosion-proof boilers and bought much lighter engines, reducing the combined boiler and engine weight to only 125 pounds. Because the Stanleys were still using light buggy chassis, the two new steamers proved to be relatively fast automobiles.

The twins entered F.E.'s car in a race at Charles River Park in Cambridge in November, 1898, to find out just how fast it really was. The oval track, used mostly for bicycle races, was a third of a mile around, and the little Stanley with both brothers aboard did three laps in two minutes and eleven seconds. This was an average speed of over twenty-seven miles an hour, an unofficial world's record at the time. Besides being the fastest car on the track that day, the Stanley steamer also won the hill-climbing contest, chugging up grades that none of the other vehicles present could manage.

The spectators were much impressed by this performance, crowding around to stare at the car and ask questions about its construction and operation. The story of the Stanleys' success continued to spread in the weeks that followed, and the twins eventually received more than two hundred offers to buy the steamer.

Although F.O. had sold his car for $600 shortly after it was completed, the twins had been experimenting with automobiles out of sheer curiosity until this point. They were not about to overlook a good business opportunity, however. In January of 1899, they bought the former bicycle plant next to their dry-plate factory in Newton, formed the Stanley Motor Carriage Company, and started to build a hundred or so cars similar to the Cambridge model. This was the first time that a large number of identical automobiles had been offered for sale in the United States.

In 1898 F. O.'s Stanley was the first car up Mt. Washington, taking over two hours to make the climb. By 1904 this Stanley, shown at the summit, was able to make the run in a bit over twenty-eight minutes with F. E. at the steering lever. Note the steam engine underneath the rear of the car.

That August, a Stanley became the first automobile to climb Mount Washington in New Hampshire, the highest peak in New England. Accompanied by his wife, F.O. drove one of the first production cars ten miles up the rugged 6,288-foot mountain in two hours and ten minutes. About a mile from the rocky summit, the car ran low on water, but a man brought a milk-can full down from the top of the mountain with a carriage and a team of horses, and the Stanley was able to complete its climb. This was at a time when other cars usually broke down repeatedly during short trips on the level, and the widespread publicity that resulted brought even more orders to the busy Stanley factory.

2 / *Yankee Competitors*

THE STANLEY BROTHERS had not planned on becoming automotive manufacturers until so many people asked to buy one of their first cars. Just as abruptly, in the spring of 1899, they suddenly sold the recently established business to John Brisben Walker, publisher of *Cosmopolitan* magazine.

Walker, a horseless-carriage enthusiast who had sponsored the second automobile race held in this country, between New York City and Irvington-on-Hudson in 1896, was convinced that steam cars were the coming thing. After riding in a Stanley and deciding that the company would be an excellent investment, he asked F.E. and F.O. to sell him half the business. According to F.O., the twins were as startled as if he had offered to buy "half interest in our wives," and they told him—probably without smiling—that they already had enough trouble getting along with each other without adding a third partner.

Walker then began to talk about the advertising advantages his magazine could offer the company, but since the Stanleys did not approve of advertising, this made the deal even less likely. The disappointed publisher went back to New York, only to return in a few months with a new idea: he would buy the entire Stanley automobile operation—factory, machinery, pending patents and all.

F.E. and F.O. decided to discourage Walker by naming a price so large that he could not meet it. They had spent less than $20,000 setting up the company, but they asked him for $250,000 in cash, to be paid within ten days! When he quickly accepted these terms, they must have been astonished indeed.

Walker set about raising the required quarter of a million dollars and asked that one of the twins bring a Stanley to New York and demonstrate the car to possible investors. F.O. agreed and drove to Providence, Rhode Island, where he put the automobile on a boat for New York City. The other passengers applauded loudly when he slowly steamed down the gangplank in Manhattan, but the trip through the heavy horse-and-wagon traffic on lower Broadway was not nearly as pleasant; F.O. called it "one of the most perilous journeys I had ever taken in my life." Both the frightened horses and their drivers regarded the steamer with great suspicion and gave it little room to pass. Nevertheless, the small car "alternately slowed down to accommodate itself to the jam of carriages, or, seizing its opportunity, darted swiftly into the openings as they presented themselves," to quote one of Mr. Walker's advertisements; and in this way F.O. managed to survive the crush.

Farther up Broadway, a girl on a bicycle ran into the side of the Stanley at full speed. While she was not hurt, she was thrown up into the seat of the car and her bicycle was completely wrecked. A crowd quickly gathered, and some angry bystanders began to threaten F.O., but a policeman who had seen the collision restored order by explaining that the girl had been looking back over her shoulder at the time she hit the car and was to blame for the accident.

F.O. arrived at Irvington, where Walker lived, without further incident, and later gave rides to a number of wealthy men, all of whom said they enjoyed the trips immensely but all of whom also hesitated at investing money in a steam-carriage company. Walker then interested William Rockefeller in the project and decided that he would himself drive Rockefeller from Irvington to Tarrytown. Not only would Rockefeller see how well the car ran, the two men could discuss financial matters in privacy along the way.

The only drawback to this idea was that Walker had never driven the car before. But a steam automobile is relatively easy to control once it has been fired up, and F.O. finally agreed to the plan, although with some uneasiness. After watching the car climb the hill near the Irvington railroad station and glide from sight, he was convinced that Walker could at least work the steering lever; and he went to talk with Walker's son.

He was startled to hear that the young man had seen water leaking from the parked car earlier and had turned off the valve between the water tank and water pump. This meant that water was no longer leaving the tank, and a scorched boiler was likely before very long. The resourceful F.O. had young Walker telephone ahead to a drug store on his father's route and ask the druggist to run out into the road and stop the car as it passed. F.O. then explained to Walker over the phone about opening the valve again, and the demonstration/conference proceeded, although Walker admitted afterwards that he was so frightened that he could barely talk. Rockefeller had a ride with F.O. as well, but he too decided against investing in the company, perhaps as a result of the boiler adventure.

Finally, on the last of the ten days that had been agreed to, Walker brought a well-off paving contractor, Amzi L. Barber, to see the Stanley. Barber was highly impressed by the steam car—so impressed, in fact, that he bought a half interest from Walker for $250,000, the entire amount that Walker was to pay F.E. and F.O. The transfer of the business from the Stanleys to Walker and Barber was then completed, and the next day F.O., accompanied by Walker's son, drove the steamer from Irvington back to Newton, another long automobile trip for 1899.

Walker and Barber renamed their expensive purchase the Automobile Company of America but soon changed to the Locomobile Company of America to avoid confusion with another organization having the same name. Although they talked grandly of setting up branch factories in England, France and Germany, their association was to be a short one, and within a few weeks they suffered what an automobile magazine politely called a "partition of interests." Barber stayed with the Locomobile Company, and Walker started his own Mobile Company of America in Tarrytown. Under the provisions of the original sale, F.E. and F.O. were general managers of both companies for one year, and during this period they could not manufacture steam cars of their own.

After this interval they completely redesigned their car and obtained a new set of patents, encountering a legal problem in the process. In those days, rear axles of automobiles were driven by chains much like bicycles, and the Stanleys had sold Walker and Barber the patent on their device for adjusting the tension of the chain drive.

This 1899 advertisement for the Locomobile Company of America lists the Stanleys as "General Managers." As claimed, no "sanitary arrangements" were required, but the car really needed more care than the stated "few moments' attention...without so much as removing your cuffs."

To avoid a lawsuit threatened by the Locomobile Company, F.E. and F.O. decided to discard chain drive and try gearing the engine directly to the rear axle of the new car. This method turned out to be more efficient than the original scheme and became standard for Stanleys from then on.

The new Stanley was also improved in many other ways over the original model still being manufactured by the Mobile and Locomobile companies. Neither organization had been doing very well anyway; and Walker and Barber apparently realized their outdated cars would not be as popular as the Stanleys' new steamers. In any event, they sold the entire steam-car business back to F.E. and F.O. at a huge loss. (The return of the patents involved was a subject of lengthy negotiation and did not take place until three years later.)

Shrewd Yankee businessmen, F.E. and F.O. had sold their business for $250,000, waited a short time and bought it back for $20,000. Since Barber had built an addition to the factory in the meantime, and the twins were eventually able to sell two of their recovered patents to another company for $15,000, they showed a profit of over a quarter of a million dollars on the transaction. In 1904 they sold their flourishing dry-plate business to the Eastman Kodak Company for an even larger sum and were thus able to concentrate on producing steam cars with a considerable financial reserve. The Mobile Company had been dissolved shortly after the sale to the Stanleys, but the Locomobile Company moved to Bridgeport, Connecticut, and later became well known as the manufacturer of fast and luxurious gasoline automobiles.

About this time F.O. became ill with tuberculosis. His doctor advised him to move to Denver for the climate, and from then on he spent at least his summers in Colorado. He later built a home in what is now the Rocky Mountain National Park and was also the owner of the Stanley Hotel there. To get the guests up to the hotel from the railroad station, the twins designed the Stanley Mountain Wagon, a forerunner of today's station wagon.

Steam-powered of course, the big red Mountain Wagons carried nine—later twelve—passengers in rows of three and were able to climb any grade where there was enough traction for their tires. Popular with resort hotels in the East as well, many of the Wagons had elaborate folding canvas tops and side curtains for running in bad weather. A Stanley Mountain Wagon sold for about $3,000 in its day, but a 1912 model brought $31,000 at auction in 1967, then a record price for an antique car.

While F.O. was in the West, F.E., who had been responsible for the greater part of the design of the earlier cars, remained in Newton to carry on at the factory. Although the brothers still scorned ordinary forms of advertising, they believed that good showings by Stanleys in speed events helped to sell automobiles, and F.E. continued to enter cars in many hill climbs and races.

In a hill climb on Commonwealth Avenue, Newton, in April, 1903, a five-and-a-half-horsepower Stanley was pitted against many larger gasoline cars, including Packards, a Cadillac and a twenty-horsepower Winton. The rules that day required a passenger in each car, and F.E. decided to let his nine-year-old son, Raymond, ride with driver Frank Durbin because the boy weighed much less than an adult, which would make the car faster. An excited Raymond climbed up to the buggy seat, crouched beside the man at the steering lever, and held on tightly as they approached the starting line.

Little clouds of steam drifted from behind the wheezing Stanley as Raymond and Durbin kept their eyes on the starter. His signal came at last. Durbin pushed the throttle open, and the car sprang silently forward, accelerating rapidly even by today's standards. Up the grade it rushed, puffing and swaying, and many of the spectators lining the road pressed closer for a better look.

Accustomed to the slower gasoline automobiles that had been competing earlier, some onlookers pushed so far into the road that Durbin had to brake in the middle of the slope, spoiling the run. The starter allowed the Stanley to return to the bottom of the hill for a second attempt,

Frank Durbin prepares to race a Stanley in Florida. This model was called the "Gentlemen's Speedy Roadster."

and once again Raymond clutched the side of the open car as it sped quickly away. This time the crowd was more cautious, and the steamer reached the top of the hill in less than seventeen seconds, ten seconds faster than the best previous time. F.E., Durbin and, of course, Raymond were delighted by the victory, but Raymond's mother, who had been watching the competition from a distance, was not nearly as pleased when she learned who the passenger had been.

Although the winner of the Commonwealth Avenue hill climb was a stock model Stanley, the first of a series of special racing cars was also built in 1903. A racing Stanley had a larger boiler and engine than a production model, but its most striking feature was a long and low-slung streamlined body, compared by some reporters to an upside-down canoe. Not much higher than their fragile bicycle-type wheels, the Stanley racers were usually painted red and had many nicknames, ranging from "Whistling Billy" to "Flying Teakettle." They were most frequently called "Wogglebugs," "Bugs" and "Beetles."

The first Bug was raced at the Readville track, near Boston, on Memorial Day, 1903, with designer F.E. in its deep cockpit. The expected competition from a Grout steamer, built in Orange, Massachusetts, and said to be capable of more than sixty miles an hour, did not develop; but the Stanley was hard pressed by another steam car designed, built and partially driven by a Harvard junior named George Cannon. ("partially driven" because the unusual Cannon required a crew of two drivers: one at the front to steer and another at the rear to operate the steam controls, throttle and brakes.)

The race between the Cannon and the Stanley was so spirited that both steamers went faster than any car had ever gone on a U.S. track. In beating the Cannon by two seconds, the Stanley set a new American record for the

A Stanley Bug trails steam as it races on the sands of Ormond Beach, Florida.

mile—1 minute, 2.8 seconds (57.3 m.p.h.)—but the record lasted only a few hours. Later that day in Yonkers, New York, the famous race driver Barney Oldfield did a mile with a Ford racer in 1 minute, 1.6 seconds (58.4 m.p.h.) to break F.E.'s record. It should be noted, however, that the gasoline-engined Ford was listed at eighty horsepower, while the Stanley steamer was rated at only ten.

3 / *The Wogglebugs on Ormond Beach*

By the beginning of this century, the east coast of Florida had already become a fashionable wintering spot for wealthy Americans; and a number of rich and socially powerful automotive enthusiasts had settled in Ormond Beach, just north of Daytona Beach. Before long these men were talking of racing their expensive cars, many of which had been imported from Europe, on the several miles of smooth wide beach edging the Atlantic between the two resorts. A group of local hotel owners enthusiastically backed the plan for it would mean much publicity for that section of the coast; and the first Tournament of Speed was held on the Ormond-Daytona Beach in April, 1902.

That first season there were only three competitors, two automobiles and a motorcycle, but in 1903 the event was officially recognized by the American Automobile Association; and it gained rapidly in number of entrants and importance every year after that. Several races were run over the hard sands south of the Ormond Hotel during each meet, and time was also scheduled for the attempts of individual automobiles at setting U.S. and international speed records.

French cars had been first to compete for the World Land Speed Record because France was the first country to build automobiles in any quantity and to race them. The earliest record holders were a pair of French electric cars that took the record away from each other five times in 1888 and 1889. A French Serpollet steam car driven by its designer was next to hold the Land Speed Record when it averaged 75.06 m.p.h. for the flying kilometer (about five eighths of a mile) in April, 1902. Serpollet lost his record in August to a French Mors, driven at 76.08 m.p.h. by William K. Vanderbilt, Jr., an American millionaire who raced automobiles in Europe and sponsored the famous Vanderbilt Cup road races in this country. The Mors was the first gasoline car to hold the Land Speed Record.

In January of 1904, the Land Speed Record came to the United States for the first time when none other than Henry Ford drove his crude but powerful Arrow racer over a frozen Michigan lake at a top speed of 91.37 m.p.h. for the mile. The record gained much valuable publicity for the recently organized Ford Motor Company in this country, but was not recognized by the French at the time. It lasted less than three weeks, in any case, and Ford himself was at Ormond Beach later in the month when William Vanderbilt, Jr., pushed the limit to 92.3 m.p.h. in a big German Mercedes.

The next year a Stanley Wogglebug racing car appeared on Ormond Beach during Speed Week. Powered by two engines and driven by Louis S. Ross, a wealthy sportsman, the twenty-horsepower steamer reached 94.73 m.p.h. for the mile. While this was faster than Vanderbilt's ninety-horsepower Mercedes of the previous season and fast enough to win the one-mile race in 1905, it was not a new record because two Frenchmen had already passed the hundred-mile mark in the meantime.

The record breaking in Florida that winter was done by Arthur Macdonald, an Englishman, at the wheel of a Napier brought from England especially for the event. In spite of rough spots in the sand, Macdonald managed a run of 104.65 m.p.h. As soon as he had finished, the huge Mercedes of Boston manufacturer Herbert L. Bowden was pushed to the starting area. Called "Flying Dutchman II," the car had been greatly lengthened to allow room for the installation of a second Mercedes engine borrowed from Bowden's motorboat. Bowden and his two-engined giant beat Macdonald's time by more than five miles an hour, but the record was not recognized in this country because of the additional weight of the "Dutchman." And, as usual, neither Macdonald's nor Bowden's record was recognized in France because they had been set outside the country.

In January, 1906, F.E. Stanley brought his family and a team of "factory" racing steamers south for the annual Ormond-Daytona trials. The team included at least one of the two cars that had originally been built for Vanderbilt Cup racing but were not accepted because the Vanderbilts' organizers mistakenly thought their steam exhausts might burn other drivers. And there was also a new Wogglebug, still looking like an upside-down red canoe on wheels and still steered by a lever, but now rated at fifty horsepower.

The Bug was entered in the first event of the meet, the one-mile Dewar Cup race, competing against an 80-horsepower English Napier and a 110-horsepower Italian Fiat. Driver of the new Beetle was Fred H. Marriott, the head of the Stanley repair department, a mechanic for F.E. and F.O. since they had first started manufacturing cars, and the man who told them apart by telling them jokes. Despite fog and drizzle during the Dewar race, Marriott and the Bug left the more powerful European cars far behind, averaging 111.8 m.p.h. The next day they set a new record for the five-mile race, as well; and the Stanley team regarded these victories as encouraging preliminaries to their Land Speed Record attempt scheduled later that week.

Some spectators, many contestants and much of the press resented the success of the unusual steam car, calling it unsafe and a freak. Even the race officials favored the gasoline cars according to Raymond Stanley, and he has written that the starting time for the thirty-mile event was suddenly advanced from 9:00 to 7:00 A.M. after his father had gone to bed the night before the race.

But F.E. had been an early riser since the days when he and F.O. were at the factory before the workmen, and he was up in time to notice the change in a posted announcement. He hurriedly got up steam in the Bug, dragged Fred Marriott out of bed, and they arrived at the starting line only a few minutes after the other cars had left. In spite of the late start, Marriott eventually caught up with the rest of the field, passed it, and won the race by three minutes.

F.E. also competed on Ormond Beach himself at times, and once drove a Vanderbilt Stanley in a match race against another uncommon automobile, the front-wheel-drive racer of Walter Christie. Raymond, then about twelve, was F.E.'s passenger during the race, but he forgot to wear goggles and has said that the sand thrown up by the Christie's wheels made his face look like a raw beet. He covered his face with his hands to avoid the stinging sand and did not see much of the race, but the steamer beat the Christie easily.

The 1906 meet came to its climax for the Stanleys on Friday, January 26. It was cloudy and rainy that morning, but the weather improved by afternoon when the record attempt was planned. Thousands of spectators were clustered about the starting area and scattered along the dunes on the land side of the one-mile course as Fred Marriott prepared the Bug for its important trial.

Much different looking from gasoline-powered racers, the Wogglebug was low, razor-nosed and, for its day, highly streamlined. In place of the heavy wooden wheels used by the other competitors, the Stanley ran on light, spidery wheels; and the driver nestled in a deep cockpit with only his head in sight, instead of being seated in the open. Behind the cockpit was a stubby stovepipe to exhaust the spent steam.

However, for most people at Ormond Beach, the biggest difference between the Stanley Bug and the other automobiles was not appearance, but sound. The gasoline cars thundered and roared along the sand, but the steamer made very little noise, and a short distance from the speeding Beetle there was only mysterious silence.

Marriott drove several miles above the starting line, turned around and began to accelerate, slowly at first. Faster and faster he went, steam streaming from behind his head, and, by the time he rocketed across the starting line and tripped the electric timing devices, he was at full throttle. The Bug shot away down the beach, spectators along the way snapping their heads from left to right as the red car blurred quietly past them. It was all over quickly, and, when Marriott streaked over the finish line, he had become the fastest man on wheels. Not only had he broken the world land speed record in a "steam freak," he had raised the record to 127.66 m.p.h. for the flying

Fred Marriott and the 1906 Wogglebug at Ormond Beach.

Marriott at speed, Ormond Beach, 1906.

mile, over two miles a minute and an astounding increase of eighteen miles an hour over the previous record.

On a second and slower run, he also set a new record for the flying kilometer, 121.57 m.p.h. Both records were immediately recognized in this country, but only the kilometer record was recognized in Paris.

Not content to stop with this accomplishment, F.E. and Marriott spent the next fall improving the engine of the record-holding car and installing a boiler that would stand greater steam pressure. When late January of 1907 came around, they were back at Ormond Beach, anxious to try for new records.

Although the sand had been badly rippled by a strong wind and speeds were rather slow on the first day, the early races went quite well for the New Englanders. Frank Durbin, who had driven the Commonwealth Avenue hill climb with Raymond as a passenger, won the mile race for touring cars in a stock Stanley, and Marriott won the five-mile race with the red Bug. On Wednesday, all three Stanleys (two Vanderbilt racers and the Bug) broke down during the ten-mile race and had to be towed back to the garage; but on Thursday the Stanley luck turned again, and F.E. set a one-mile record for steam touring cars.

When the tide went out on Friday, the beach seemed in better condition, and Marriott decided to go ahead with the attempt at breaking his own record. The year before he had done the flying mile in 28 1/5 seconds, but his first run in 1907 was a relatively slow 32 4/5 seconds. He tried again and got down to 29 3/5 seconds, still not nearly fast enough. He stopped to explain to F. E. that the problem was two small ripples in the sand at one point, and is reported to have said, "The next time I'll hit those ripples so fast I'll skim right over them without even feeling them."

Once again Marriott drove well past the starting area, turned around, and whistled toward the line. Past the starter he flew, speeding down the beach faster than he had ever done before—until he hit those two ripples in the sand. The nose of the steamer bounced high off the beach, and the pressure of the air got underneath the closed bottom of the car, lifting it even higher. The Stanley traveled over a hundred feet on only its rear wheels, veered, and then crashed heavily on its side, rolling over in a great cloud of steam. The Bug was completely smashed, its wooden body shattered into small pieces, and the hissing boiler rolled down the beach for several hundred feet. Marriott was thrown into the surf and badly hurt, but he recovered completely in a short time.

Fred Marriott, head of the Stanley repair department and holder of the World Land Speed Record, 1906-1910.

Front view of the record-holding Stanley. The large pipe behind Marriott's head is the steam exhaust.

There was no official evidence of the speed of the Bug at the time of the accident, and there has been considerable discussion about it ever since. Much later, when Marriott was over eighty, he told a writer that he was doing 197 when he hit the hollows in the beach; but it seems likely that his memory had improved on the car's ability over the years. The best indication we have is some figures of F.E.'s, based on a stop-watch reading and his measurement of the distance from the starting line to the place where the Bug hit the ripples. According to F.E.'s arithmetic, the car was traveling at a rate of 150 m.p.h. and would certainly have set a remarkable new record had it not crashed.

The Stanleys were so upset by Marriott's injuries they never raced again. But they had already advanced the Land Speed Record by such a large amount that their 1906 mark stood for over four years during a period when automobile speed records sometimes changed hands in a matter of days. Then, in March of 1910, Barney Oldfield finally broke Marriott's record by doing 131.72 m.p.h. in the gasoline-engined Blitzen Benz at Ormond-Daytona, and a steam car had held the World Land Speed Record for the last time.

4 / *End of the Road*

THEIR RACING DAYS behind them, the Stanleys now concentrated on manufacturing sturdy and reliable steam automobiles for the general public, producing about six hundred cars a year. Their 1908 catalog listed a little ten-horsepower runabout, twenty- and thirty-horsepower touring cars, the "Gentlemen's Speedy Roadster" (twenty horsepower) and a limousine, first built as a special model for F.E.'s wife. A Model K Semi-Racer (thirty horsepower), "entirely practical for everyday use," was also available in limited numbers even though the factory was no longer engaged in competition.

Prices for these cars ranged from $850 for the runabout to $2,500 for the limousine, moderately expensive for the time. A bulb horn and a pair of kerosene lamps came with each automobile, but speedometers, folding cloth tops and acetylene gas lamps were extra. The Stanleys looked much like the other automobiles of that period, with high open bodies, big wooden wheels with thin tires, and primitive fenders, then called mud guards. They were much different from gasoline cars mechanically, however.

When the tub-shaped hood of a Stanley was lifted, there

This Stanley roadster has been stripped of its fenders and lights for competition. Note the characteristic tub-shaped hood which covers the boiler.

was no engine in sight, only a great deal of plumbing and an asbestos-covered boiler that looked like a large but somewhat dirty marshmallow. The maze of piping brought water from a big tank under the front seat into the boiler, and also carried kerosene from another large tank at the back of the car to a burner under the boiler. The burner, a large-sized version of the Bunsen burners used in school laboratories, heated water in the boiler to make steam, which was then piped to the engine underneath the rear of the car. The steam engine, much like those of steam locomotives except for its size, was smaller and simpler than a gasoline engine and was geared directly to the rear axle without a transmission. In later, condensing-model Stanleys, the steam was next brought forward to the front of the car, passed through a radiator to cool and condense it back to water, then ran by gravity back to the water tank and circulated all over again. In the earlier models, the exhausted steam trailed behind the car and on cool days often formed a foggy cloud which made it impossible for following drivers to see the road, much less the Stanley.

Driving a Stanley was quite simple, particularly as compared to handling the complicated controls of gasoline cars of that day. There was no carburetion to worry about, no ignition "spark" to adjust, no clutch pedal to push, and no gears to be shifted. For Stanley drivers, there was only a steering wheel, a throttle lever under the wheel, a brake

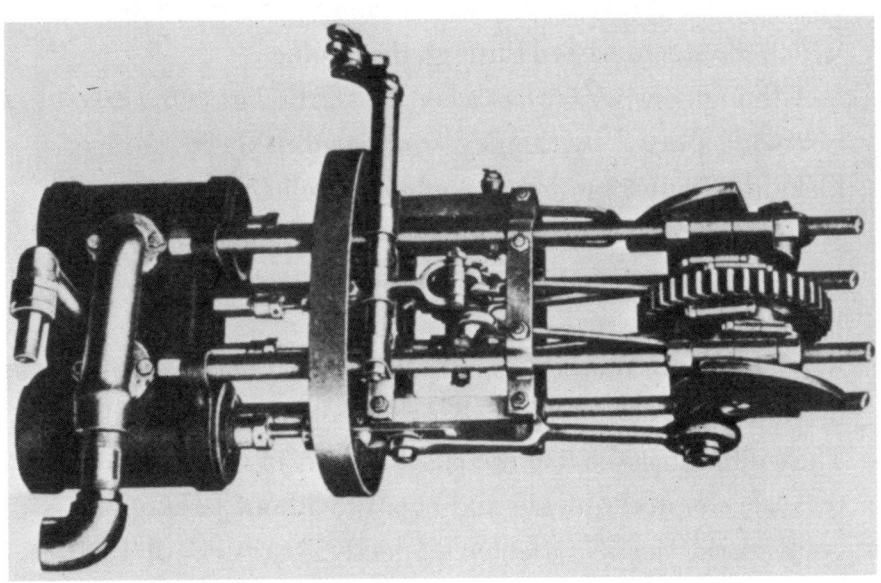

Seen here from above, the Stanley engine contained only thirteen moving parts and thus wore much less rapidly than gasoline engines. Steam was piped from the boiler at the front of the car to the steam chest at the left of the photograph. The expansive force of the steam moved two pistons inside the chest, and they turned the large gear at the right by means of the linkage in the center of the illustration. The engine was underneath the rear of the car and geared directly to the rear axle.

pedal for the right foot and a reverse pedal for the left foot. The throttle controlled the amount of steam reaching the engine, and the reverse pedal changed the direction in which the steam passed through the engine.

Although one writer has recorded startled gasoline drivers being passed by Stanleys running briskly in reverse, kicking a Stanley into reverse while traveling at high speed would probably have ruined the engine. A more common trick was using the reverse pedal to help the Stanley's weak brakes stop the car.

Backward or forward, Stanleys were fast and smooth to drive, even when compared to present-day automobiles. They did not shake like the gasoline cars of the time, and they accelerated quickly and evenly without jerking. On good roads, the "Gentlemen's Speedy Roadster" of 1908 was capable of seventy miles an hour, and 1914 Stanleys were reported as being able to accelerate from zero to sixty miles an hour in eleven seconds. (A well-tuned Triumph sports car does it today in about ten.)

Because of performance figures like these, it was often said that the twins would pay $1,000—or give a new car—to anyone who could hold one of their cars at full throttle for three minutes. While no such offer was ever really made, the legend is still being widely circulated and is the first thing most people say when they see a Stanley.

Stanleys could also climb better than gasoline cars,

would not stall at awkward moments, and were much quieter in operation. They cost less to run, as well, for kerosene was much cheaper than gasoline. And some enterprising owners even discovered they could roast peanuts on top of the boiler while the car was in motion!

In spite of all these advantages, by 1916 there were only 799 Stanleys registered in Massachusetts as compared to 30,871 Fords. Twenty-six makes of gasoline automobiles exceeded Stanleys in numbers of registrations in their home state. What had happened?

The first reason was unjustified fear. Many horrible stories about Stanley boiler explosions are still going around, but the fact is they never happened. Every Stanley boiler was wrapped with three layers of piano wire so that the interior tubes would leak harmlessly long before the outside casing exploded; there was a safety valve on the boiler in any case; and other valves shut off water and fuel automatically once a certain boiler pressure was reached. Stanleys were usually operated at a maximum steam pressure of six hundred pounds per square inch on the road, but F.E. and F.O. once buried a boiler in the vacant lot next to the factory and got it up to fifteen hundred pounds before the tubes leaked. While there was no danger or risk with a wound boiler, when the twins repeated their experiment with an unwound boiler, it *did* explode at twelve hundred pounds, shattering every window on that side of the factory.

In spite of these demonstrations and F.O.'s attempts at educational humor—he liked to surprise onlookers by secretly dropping big firecrackers under the boiler while he got up steam—many people were still afraid of Stanleys. Perhaps they didn't explode, after all, but weren't they always catching fire?

Driving a Stanley was relatively simple, but getting up steam involved the careful operation of several valves and keeping a sharp eye on a number of gauges.

Well, not exactly. Unwary drivers sometimes allowed the burner to flood, which caused spectacular flames to leap from beneath the hood. The front of the car had been designed as a fireproof compartment for just such incidents, however, and the solution was to turn off the fuel and wait till the fire went out of its own accord. (With steam up, a Stanley could run for two or three miles after the fuel had been shut off.) But fire departments did not always understand this little failing and sometimes pursued and watered down smoking Stanleys while their owners protested loudly.

The objections to the complicated method of firing up a cold Stanley must be taken more seriously. The pilot light, which burned gasoline under pressure from an air tank filled by a few strokes of the tire pump, had to be heated and lighted first; and then came lighting the burner itself. This was not always an easy task because the two jet holes in the burner's vaporizer sometimes clogged and had to be poked open with a little hook. There was also the flow of water, kerosene, gasoline and lubricating oil to control, and this meant watching several gauges and turning a number of valves in exactly the proper amounts and correct order. Experts could get up steam in fifteen minutes, but most people took half an hour, and it was a common practice to leave the pilot burning overnight to save time in the morning. In the early years, firing up a steamer took no longer than cleaning, feeding and hitching up a pair of horses, and was faster and safer than hand-cranking a gasoline automobile; but when the electric self-starter appeared on gas cars in 1911, the Stanleys were at a distinct disadvantage.

There was also the water problem. Condensing Stanleys got about ten miles to the gallon of water, and non-condensing models, only one. Earlier cars had a long hose with a strainer in the end coiled on the running board so the driver could pull up beside a pond or brook, throw out the hose, and take on a full tank of water.

An even more convenient source of water for steam cars was the horse-watering trough, found nearly everywhere in the early days of the automobile. Raymond Stanley had his own small steamer from the time he was in eighth grade, and, when he and his father once drove to Maine in separate cars, Raymond left first and chalked messages to F.E. on the horse troughs along the way. But as automobiles increased in number and horses grew fewer, there were not as many horse troughs and not as many places for Stanleys to get water.

Little things also bothered many otherwise-possible Stanley owners. The burner often made an unpleasant howling and groaning noise when it was warming up, for one thing. Ferryboats refused to carry Stanleys with lit pilots because of the danger of fire, for another. And there was also the matter of the odor—even away from their cars,

Stanley owners were easily recognized because they always smelled slightly of kerosene.

None of these drawbacks bothered true steam men in the slightest, but by now the automobile industry had outgrown the days of the wealthy enthusiast and was building cars for the general public. While Stanleys were still being

Owners of restored Stanleys use propane torches to heat the pilot light and also to light the pilot.

hand-built in small numbers, no two cars ever being exactly the same, the large factories in Detroit were already turning out large quantities of identical gasoline automobiles. These mass-produced cars were not only much cheaper, they were also heavily advertised and sold on the installment plan as well, sales methods that the Stanleys regarded as virtually immoral. By 1914 Henry Ford was making more cars in a day than the Stanleys did in a year; but the brothers would not change their way of doing business and were thus themselves the greatest reason for the decline of the steamer. At the same time that new methods of production and distribution brought down the cost of gasoline cars, the prices of hand-built Stanleys went up and reduced their market even further.

"We know there is more money in gas cars," the brothers were once quoted as saying. "Just the same, steamers are a lot more fun." The Stanleys had fun driving their cars as well as building them, and they drove very rapidly. There are stories about one twin being stopped for speeding and the other flashing by in an identical car to confuse the police; and F.E. once pleaded not guilty when charged with driving sixty miles an hour because he said he was doing eighty-seven at the time.

Both brothers retired from the Stanley Motor Carriage Company in 1917, when they were sixty-eight, but they continued their extensive range of activities and interests. Among his other projects, F.E. invented a steam "unit-car" to replace trolleys; and on July 31, 1918, he was driving his steamer along the Newburyport Turnpike on his way to a conference about its development.

Just as he sped over the brow of a hill, he saw two farmers blocking the road with their wagons. Rather than hit and

F. E. Stanley in his later years.

injure them, he chose to crash into a woodpile. He was badly injured and died shortly afterwards.

F.O. never fully recovered from this shock, although he lived to be ninety-one, returning to the manufacture of violins with a cousin. By 1923 the reorganized Stanley company was in severe financial trouble, and it collapsed entirely in 1925.

The White steamer, closest rival to the Stanley in its heyday, was also out of production by this time. The White Motor Company, originally a manufacturer of sewing machines, built steamers between 1901 and 1911, then switched to gasoline cars until 1918. (It now makes trucks and busses.) Altogether, more than one hundred and twenty different kinds of steam automobiles were once made in this country; but by the First World War the steamers were vastly outnumbered, and gasoline cars ruled the road. Among the last of the steamers, and probably the best, was the extremely high-quality Doble, perhaps two dozen of which were made in the late twenties. A Doble would fire up within forty-five seconds of turning a key in the dash, but few could afford the $9,000 price.

During World War II, gasoline was rationed, and a number of old steam cars, including many Stanleys, reappeared on U. S. highways and ran very well. People noticed how smoothly they accelerated, how economical they were to operate, and that their engines did not wear as rapidly as those of gasoline cars. The question of building up-to-date steamers was soon raised and has cropped up occasionally since then.

Until recently, the possibility that any U.S. manufacturer would ever turn out steam cars again seemed slight, but our worsening air-pollution situation has somewhat increased the chances for a steam revival. Even though automotive engineers have been successful in greatly reducing the amount of injurious material given off by gasoline engines, they are also considering other ways of powering automobiles once again. Most of their attention so far has been directed at electric cars, but the major problem of F.E. and F.O.'s day still exists: getting batteries that are capable of holding enough energy for a long trip, yet are small and light enough to be carried in the car without slowing it down, especially on hills.

Steam-powered automobiles pollute the air only very slightly as compared to gasoline cars and do not have a battery difficulty. Therefore, two Senate committees have recently conducted a joint inquiry into the possibility of replacing our gasoline vehicles with steamers, and both Ford and General Motors have shown some interest in developing experimental steam cars of late. The automotive industry continues to strongly favor gasoline cars, however, mostly because of its huge investment in them.

Several individuals have assembled modern-day steam

Stanleys never fail to attract enthusiastic crowds at antique car meets.

cars, nevertheless, including one man who uses steam to power his 1958 Volkswagen. Best known of today's steamers is the Williams, a sporty red and white roadster put together on a 1950 Ford chassis by the Williams brothers of Ambler, Pennsylvania. Like the Stanleys, Calvin and Charles Williams are twins. Their car is much more advanced, of course. It will start in twenty seconds, develop a full head of steam in less than a minute, and can do a hundred miles an hour. The Williams gets twenty-five miles to a gallon of kerosene and fifty miles per gallon of water.

But even if there is no serious consideration of the steamer as everyday transportation again, Stanleys will continue to fascinate the crowds at antique car meets for a long time to come. And each time that one is shown, someone will be certain to say, "Say, did you know there was a standing offer of a thousand dollars to anyone who could hold the throttle wide open for three minutes?"

III
CLASSIC CARS

Acknowledgments

THE AUTHOR WISHES TO THANK the following for their help in preparing this book:

John W. Burgess, Sr., Director-Manager, Briggs Cunningham Automotive Museum, Costa Mesa, Ca.; the Classic Car Club of America; Dave Dennison, Press Information Manager, Mercedes-Benz of North America, Inc.; Henry E. Edmunds, Director, Ford Archives, Henry Ford Museum, Dearborn, Mi.; James W. Edwards, Services Supervisor, Harrah's Automobile Collection, Reno, Nv.; J. R. Mauller, Manager, Early American Museum, Silver Springs, Fl.; Thomas I. H. Powel, Southport, Ct.; Joel Schointuch, Advertising Manager, Life-Like Products, Inc.; and Judith H. Sussman, Marketing Services Coordinator, Gabriel Industries, Inc.

Photographs are reproduced by courtesy of the following: Briggs Cunningham Automotive Museum, pages 131, 139 and 155; Mercedes-Benz of North America, Inc., page 133; Thomas I. H. Powel, page 141; Early American Museum, pages 144 and 161; Hubley Division, Gabriel Industries, Inc., page 150; Harrah's Automobile Collection, page 153; Ford Archives, page 165.

Other photographs are by the author.

1 / *Majestic Giants of the Past*

SMELLING OF LEATHER AND OIL, swift and elegant, the big luxury cars of the late twenties and thirties represent the best of fine automobiles. Majestic giants of the past like the American Duesenberg, English Bentley, French Hispano-Suiza and Italian Isotta-Fraschini now bring much higher prices than when they were new because of this excellence in combination with their scarcity.

Such cars were produced late enough in the development of the automobile to have all the basic mechanical features of current mass-produced cars. In addition, however, they were built at a time when the individuality, distinguished design and workmanship of automobiles made entirely by hand was still economically possible. Therefore these automobiles have set standards against which all other cars must be judged, and they are called "classic cars" as a result.

But "classic" is a word that has been used so widely and so loosely that it has lost some of its meaning; and it is not a particularly exact word when used to describe an automobile, anyway. For these reasons some disagreement exists among the experts as to just which cars deserve to be called classic.

The best authority is the Classic Car Club of America, an organization of some four thousand admirers and collectors who are highly dedicated to the preservation of classic cars. According to their definition a classic car must have been made between 1925 and 1942. These specific dates were chosen because by 1925 all the basic mechanical features of today's cars (such as four-wheel brakes) had been introduced, and in 1942 U.S. automobile production was stopped because of World War II. None of the cars made after the war meet the Classic Car Club of America's other standards except the Lincoln Continentals of 1946-48.

For the CCCA has also ruled that a classic car must have been a limited-production luxury automobile with special technical features, and not have been strictly mass-produced. Mass-produced cars can be turned out quickly in large numbers and sold for far less than handmade automobiles, but cars manufactured on fast-moving production lines must have many compromises made in their design and quality.

In contrast classic cars were made slowly, one at a time, with virtually no regard for time, trouble or cost. Painstakingly constructed by the most skilled craftsmen available, from the finest materials to be had, to the exacting specifications of the best designers, they were as close to perfection in every aspect as was humanly possible.

Their technically superior and very powerful engines, for instance, were assembled with the precision of a costly watch. Noted for performance, reliability and silence, they are also almost impossible to wear out. Another difference from modern engines is that they are attractive to look at, with neat, uncluttered and highly "sanitary" engine compartments and their outside surfaces either expensively enameled or polished to mirror-brightness.

A famous demonstration by an Hispano-Suiza once proved just how well such engines were put

The large but tidy aluminum straight-eight engine of a 1930 Isotta-Fraschini 8A. Each of the two carburetors supplies gasoline to four cylinders.

together. The Hisso was driven hard over 1,100 miles from Paris to Nice and back again, then immediately parked over a large sheet of white paper. Not the slightest trace of water or oil ever dropped from the engine.

Impressive as the engines of classic cars are,

though, it is the eye-catching appearance of the mighty automobiles that turns heads to this very day. Spacious and imposing in size, the majority of classic cars are even longer than most large automobiles of the present. They are also much higher and roll on big wheels (usually wire) that are twice the diameter of current models'.

In spite of this bulk most classic cars nave tasteful lines and balanced proportions that are still strikingly handsome. At the front there is usually a huge, brightly chromed radiator, topped with an ornate cap and flanked by mammoth exposed headlights. On either side of an enormously long hood, spare wheels typically nestle in shallow wells located in the gracefully sweeping front fenders; and at the rear there is often a boxy leather-covered trunk or a big suitcase rack. As for body styles, the sports cars are apt to be open, two-seated, boat-tailed speedsters while the touring automobiles range from cabriolets (now called convertibles) to stiffly formal town cars in which the passengers are enclosed but the chauffeur drives in the open.

Much of the appeal of classic "coachwork" lies in its individuality. Most companies that built classic cars sold only a bare chassis for which the customer then arranged with a coachwork firm to design and build a custom body. (Some owners went so far as to order *two* bodies per chassis, an open body for summer and a closed style for winter.)

Stunning on the outside, these one-of-a-kind bodies are also lavishly trimmed on the inside. Upholstered in the most expensive fabrics and leathers, carpeted like a drawing room and inlaid with mahogany, walnut or rosewood, many also

Most classic cars have tasteful lines and balanced proportions that are still strikingly handsome. This is a 1928 Hispano-Suiza H6b town car.

have silk curtains at the windows for privacy. Having been built to order, they vary as to special fittings. There are cars with built-in luggage, picnic sets, bars and even toilets in the back seat, and some have telephones from the rear to the chauffeur up front. (The chauffeur or owner-driver had his special features, too; many classics are automatically lubricated by stepping on a special pedal, for example.)

All this luxury and mechanical perfection was extremely expensive, of course. At a time of economic depression when ordinary mass-produced automobiles sold for a few hundred dollars, the big limited-production classics cost many thousand. This meant that only a few of the richest people could afford them; and the original owners were usually millionaires, maharajahs or movie stars, many of whom bought their cars for snob appeal.

But over the years dedicated automotive enthusiasts such as members of the Classic Car Club of America have searched out the remaining examples of this glamorous machinery and carefully restored them so that all may appreciate their excellence. So great is the dedication of classic car fanciers, in fact, that one owner is said to have directed in his will that he be buried at the wheel of his beloved automobile.

2 / *Classic Cars From Abroad*

FRANCE

Bugatti (bōō-gŏt-tē′). Ettore Buggatti, an Italian, built his famous cars in Molsheim, a small town in eastern France, most of them between the two World Wars. Nearly everyone in Molsheim worked for him; their food was raised locally, and Bugatti had his own hotel, museum, boatyard and distillery near the factory. He even constructed his own generating plant for electricity after the local power company offended him by sending a second-notice bill.

There were also stables in Molsheim because Bugatti was an enthusiastic horseman who often wore stylish riding clothes on his morning tours of the factory. He wanted his cars to be thoroughbreds like his horses; and their radiators were shaped like a horseshoe, perhaps to symbolize this intention.

Only "Le Patron," as Bugatti liked to be called, had the keys to his buildings; and he made every important decision in Molsheim as well as most of the minor ones. He was so egotistical that he named a daughter with his initials, "L'Ebé"; and it has been said that the haughty Bugatti once refused to sell a car to the King of Albania because he dis-

approved of the King's table manners. In addition to being a crusty individualist, Bugatti was also a self-taught mechanical genius, however; and he produced six thousand or so of the world's finest automobiles.

Bugatti not only built the most successful racing cars in Europe but fast, luxurious touring automobiles as well, noted for their cornering and road-holding ability. The best of the road "Bugs" is usually thought to be the Type 57, which had an eight-cylinder engine with two overhead camshafts and was equipped with shock absorbers costing one thousand dollars a set.

The photograph shows a 57SC Bugatti at speed. "S" means a sports version, and "C" indicates that the engine has a supercharger (*compresseur* in French) pumping additional gasoline and air mixture into the cylinders for greater power. The car was constructed in 1936 for Baron Rothschild of France and when delivered it was capable of 130 mph. Its dramatic "Atlantic" coupe body was designed by Jean Bugatti, Ettore's son, who was later killed in another Type 57 while trying to avoid a postman who had ridden his bicycle onto the Molsheim test track.

The characteristically blue body of this 57SC

is made of a special lightweight aluminum alloy that could not be welded, and the unusual flanges along the hood, roof and fenders are where the body panels have been riveted together. In 1971 the car was sold for $59,000 at a Los Angeles auction, then a record price, to a Bugatti enthusiast who already owned twelve other Bugs.

Hispano-Suiza (ēs-pŏ′-no swēs′-ă). The large and stately Hispano-Suiza received its name because it was first built in Spain from the designs of a Swiss engineer, Marc Birkigt. Birkigt, who had originally left Switzerland for Spain to work on electric locomotives, became factory manager and chief designer for the Hispano-Suiza organization at the time it was formed in Barcelona in 1904. Among the company's first successes was a very early four-cylinder sports car named "Alfonso" after the King of Spain, an enthusiastic owner who was later to buy the first car of every model that Hispano-Suiza introduced.

When World War I interrupted automobile production, Hispano-Suiza turned to the manufacture of aircraft engines. Military planes were then being used for the first time, and Birkigt designed a revolutionary lightweight V-8 aviation engine that proved to be one of the best.

The "Hisso" aircraft engine powered such famous combat planes of World War I as the British SE-5, the French Spad and the French Nieuport; and it was a favorite of French ace Georges Guynemer who mysteriously disappeared while on a mission in 1917. The emblem on the sides of the planes in his squadron was a flying stork; and when Hispano-Suiza resumed making automobiles after the war every car had a small statue of a similar stork mounted on its radiator cap.

Birkigt applied many of the technical improvements he had developed for his aircraft engine to the cars he built in the twenties. One of his greatest was the Type H6, first manufactured in both Barcelona and Paris but later produced primarily in Paris alone. The photograph shows an H6c "Boulogne," named after a race in which similar cars placed first and second in 1923.

Extremely advanced mechanically, the H6 Hispano-Suiza had an enameled six-cylinder engine with two spark plugs for each cylinder and a crankshaft that was skillfully machined instead of being cast like modern versions. From a 770-pound block of the finest steel obtainable, 671 pounds were slowly ground away to make each ninety-nine-pound crankshaft. As a result of this and other costly

manufacturing methods, Hispano-Suizas were the most expensive cars on the road in their day, priced in the vicinity of $20,000.

The largest Hispano-Suiza, the twelve-cylinder Type 68 which succeeded the H6, was built in Paris from 1931 until 1938 when the company had to concentrate on military matters once more. Despite weighing nearly five thousand pounds and having a 158-inch wheelbase in its longest version, the super-luxurious Type 68 could easily top one hundred miles an hour.

Germany

Mercedes-Benz (mēr-sâd′-ēs bĕnz). Germans Gottlieb Daimler and Karl Benz are usually given credit for building the first practical gasoline motor vehicles, Benz in 1885 and Daimler in 1886. Both automotive pioneers formed companies to manufacture cars for sale; and in 1926 these firms were combined to form Daimler-Benz. By then cars built by the Daimler company had been renamed "Mercedes" for the daughter of a financial backer; and models produced by the new organization were called Mercedes-Benz.

Both factories had been active in racing before their merger; and shortly after their combination Mercedes-Benz became known throughout Europe for its "S" series of fast white sports cars. Big and high, with long, slotted hoods and a stack of two thirty-three-inch spare wheels usually mounted at the rear, the "S" cars were supercharged for extra speed; and the moaning shriek of the supercharger over the engine's loud roar is the most memorable characteristic of an "S" during brisk acceleration.

The "S" series of the Mercedes-Benz was designed by Ferdinand Porsche, who was later to design the Volkswagen "Beetle" and the first model of the sports car bearing his name. While Daimler was still independent, Porsche had first designed a rather mild Mercedes touring car and then modified his original plan to produce the Model K Mercedes. The Model K had a six-cylinder, 381-cubic-inch engine that turned out 110 horsepower without the supercharger and 160 horsepower when the "blower" was activated by tromping the accelerator to the floor. This supercharger was so powerful that it could be used for only a few seconds at a time; otherwise it would overstress the engine.

Porsche's next step was to increase the engine size of the K Mercedes to 415 cubic inches, then lower and lighten the chassis. This variation, called

the Model S, appeared in 1927 as a full-fledged Mercedes-Benz.

The S was followed by Model SS ("Sportmodell S") which had been further lightened and modified, its engine capable of a maximum of 180 horsepower. In 1928 the SSK (*kurz* is German for "short") appeared (photo), its wheelbase having been shortened from 134 to 116 inches to make it more suitable for the popular European motor sport of hill-climbing. The last—and fastest—of the fierce "S" cars were a small number of SSKL (*leicht* means "light") all-out racers, built only for use by factory teams in competition. The SSKL's, which had holes drilled everywhere, even in their frames, for still greater lightness, had big "Elephant" superchargers, were rated at three hundred horsepower, and could reach 130 mph.

Great Britain

Rolls-Royce. Even those who are not car buffs can usually recognize the formal gabled radiator and winged-lady hood ornament of a Rolls-Royce; and over the years the very words "Rolls-Royce" have become synonymous with the highest possible quality to the general public. While some experts may have reservations about current models, there is no doubt whatever that a Rolls-Royce constructed during the classic period was, just as the company's slogan stated, "The Best Car In The World."

Henry Royce was a constructor of electric cranes in Manchester, England, who did not build his first car until he was almost forty; and he did so then only because he was dissatisfied with the one he had just bought. Royce's effort turned out better than any automobile then on the market, and in 1904 he began the manufacture of Rolls-Royces for sale to others. They were given the double name because they were first sold by a London car dealer, Charles Rolls. Rolls, who was a pioneer motorist, balloonist and aviator, was associated with Royce for only six years; he was killed in a flying accident in 1910.

Royce believed in concentrating on making only one model at a time; and he insisted that every detail of every car be perfect, no matter how much difficulty or expense was involved. Until 1949 Rolls-Royce built chassis only, coachwork firms adding the bodies later, usually to the specifications of each customer. The main factory was first located in Manchester, then later moved to Derby (it is now in Crewe); but Rolls-Royces were also built in Springfield, Massachusetts, between 1920 and 1931.

From the beginning Rolls-Royces (the factory thinks it quite impolite to refer to one as merely a "Rolls") have been world-famous for exceptionally smooth and quiet operation; and their model names have reflected this characteristic. The long-lived "Silver Ghost" was produced from 1907 until 1925, its successor the "Phantom I" between 1925 and 1929, and Royce's last personal design, the "Phantom II," was made from 1929 until 1935.

Many Rolls-Royce fanciers regard the Continental short-chassis version of the Phantom II (photo) as the finest Rolls-Royce ever made. Its wheelbase measured 144 inches as compared to the usual 150. Fast yet arm-chair comfortable, the Continental Phantom II has a 468-cubic-inch engine that can take the big car up to nearly one hundred miles an hour. According to one owner, the only sound louder at that speed than at idle is the wind.

Bentley. Best known of the many sports cars produced in Great Britain during the twenties are the big, high Bentleys. Usually painted a dark green, Britain's official racing color, sporting Bentleys have folding windshields, bicycle-type fenders, and hefty brake levers mounted outside their large, tublike open bodies. Bentleys are also noted for their very strong construction, Ettore Bugatti once being so unkind as to remark that Monsieur Bentley made the fastest trucks in the world.

W. O. Bentley, a designer of aircraft engines during World War I, began to build these celebrated speedsters in 1919. The first Bentleys had three-liter (183-cubic-inch), four-cylinder engines; and variations among these three-liter Bentleys can be distinguished by the background colors of their winged "B" radiator badges. Three-liter Bentleys in standard trim are known as "Blue Label" cars, while "Red Label" Speed Models are faster, having been guaranteed by the factory to do ninety mph. Swiftest of all were the limited number of "Green Label" Super Sports three-liter Bentleys, capable of one hundred mph.

The "Big Six" Bentley, added to the line in 1926, has a larger six-cylinder 402-cubic-inch engine. While the "Big Six" was originally intended as a touring chassis suitable for luxurious closed "saloon" bodies rather than open sporting coachwork, the company's lively racing interest prevailed and a "Speed Six" version appeared before long.

Bentleys made their most memorable racing mark in the famous twenty-four-hour endurance race at Le Mans, France. Three-liter cars won there in 1924 and 1927, the sturdy 1927 winner persisting through the rain in spite of a collision that had knocked out a headlight, cracked a steering connection, twisted the chassis, and bent the front axle, to list only part of the damage.

The 1928 Le Mans race was won by a 4.5-liter (268-cubic-inch) Bentley which was similar to the three-liter car but had a bigger engine. In 1929 a "Speed Six" and three 4.5 Bentleys swept Le Mans with a crushing 1-2-3-4 finish; and in 1930 a "Speed Six" won again to give Bentley four straight victories. It was also about the same time that a group of

enthusiasts called the "Bentley Boys" supercharged a small number of 4.5 cars to produce the powerful "Blower Bentleys" (photo), fastest of them all.

A massive eight-liter (487-cubic-inch) touring Bentley was introduced by the factory in 1930, but only about a hundred were ever made. The worsening economic depression dealt a final blow to the company's already tottering finances; and in 1931 the Bentley organization was absorbed by Rolls-Royce.

ITALY

Alfa Romeo (ăl-fă′ rō-mā′-ō). A.L.F.A. stands for Anonima Lombarda Fabbrica Automobili, the Lombardy Automobile Manufacturing Company, formed in 1909 in Milan, capital of the Lombardy region of northern Italy. "Romeo" comes from industrialist Nicola Romeo, who took over the company in 1915; and since its beginning Alfa Romeo has made fine high-speed touring automobiles, sports cars and all-out racing models.

After World War I, when the Alfa factory team became prominent in European competition, one of its drivers was Enzo Ferrari, now the manufacturer of prestigious Italian sports and racing cars himself. It was Ferrari, among others, who persuaded another young man, Vittorio Jano, to leave Fiat and come to Alfa, where he was to establish his reputation as one of the foremost automotive designers in the world.

Jano's first production Alfa was the revolutionary Tipo (type) 6C of 1925 in which he completely broke away from the then-common practice of building large cars with big engines. The Alfa Romeo 6C was much shorter, lighter and lower than most other automobiles of the time because Jano had correctly reasoned that a light, low and highly

responsive car would handle better and be easier to drive.

The smaller car did not need as large an engine as its heavier rivals, and Jano's high-revving engine for the 6C also turned out more power for its size than the Alfa's big competitors. At first the engine was only 1487 cubic centimeters (91 cubic inches) in capacity, then in 1929 it was enlarged to 1752 centimeters (107 cubic inches).

Because of the car's engine size it became

known as the 1750 Alfa, and three versions of the 1750 were available. The Turismo (touring) 1750 had a wheelbase of 122 inches and was a seventy-mph car; the Gran Turismo 1750 came in either a 114- or 108-inch wheelbase and had an eighty-mph maximum speed; while the Gran Sport, built on the short 108-inch chassis, had a supercharged engine and could do ninety-five mph. No matter their speed, however, all three variations of the 1750 would stick to the road like glue.

Most desirable of the series today is considered to be the 1750GS, with a graceful roadster body in which the driver is seated almost over the rear axle (photo). During their heyday 1750GS Alfas won nearly every race they entered; and in recognition surviving examples are usually painted blood red, the international Italian racing color.

Isotta-Fraschini (ē-sōt'-ă fräs-kēn'-ē). Italy's second great car of the classic period was also manufactured in Milan; but in contrast to the little Alfa Romeo 1750 two-seater, the Isotta-Fraschini was a big, formal limousine that was usually driven by a chauffeur. Made from 1901 until 1936 by a company started by Cesare Isotta and Vincenzo Fraschini, the splendid Isotta-Fraschini was the chief rival of the French Hispano-Suiza; and many models of the two luxury cars are quite similar in appearance. An Isotta-Fraschini can be identified by its large "IF" radiator badge; and the letters are said to stand for "Intrepida Fides" (courage and loyalty) as well as the names of the makers.

Like the Hispano-Suiza organization Isotta-Fraschini manufactured aircraft engines during World War I and applied the experience to making automobiles afterwards. Concentrating on the production of only a single model, they began building the Tipo 8 in 1919.

The imposing Tipo 8 has an eight-cylinder aluminum engine, the first "straight" (cylinders in a straight line) eight to be put into production (8A engine photo, page 10). It was also equipped with four-wheel brakes, Isotta-Fraschini having been the first automobile manufacturer to standardize their use. The Tipo 8 was a very expensive car, a bare chassis alone selling for approximately $6,500 in the United States, where more Isotta-Fraschinis were purchased than in Europe. Among Tipo 8 owners in this country were such public figures as fighter Jack Dempsey, actor Rudolph Valentino and William Randolph Hearst, the newspaper publisher.

/ 143

An improved version, the Tipo 8A (photo), succeeded the 8 in 1924, and was itself replaced by the 8B in 1931. The 8B is generally thought to be the finest Isotta-Fraschini, but few were sold. Financially hard times had come with the economic crisis of the Great Depression, and there was little market for cars that were so elegant and costly. A surviving example, for instance, has polished mahogany tool boxes, trimmed in silver, mounted on its running boards. As one writer has pointed out, a buyer could get ten Buicks for the price of a single Isotta-Fraschini in the United States; and most people could not even afford a Buick.

In 1932 Henry Ford was ready to buy the struggling concern, but the Italian government did not want foreign ownership of Isotta-Fraschini and refused to allow the purchase. The declining company survived until just after World War II by increasing its manufacture of marine and aircraft engines and by making military vehicles.

3 / U.S. Classic Cars

Auburn. The Auburn 851 Speedster does not meet the usual high-cost requirement for being called a classic car because it was not very expensive originally. It does measure up to classic standards in terms of its performance and styling, however. In fact, an Auburn Speedster's price of $2,245 in 1935 was so low in comparison to the car's overall quality that it was one of the biggest automobile bargains ever offered.

The Auburn company, located in Auburn, Indiana, first built cars in 1900 but did not produce particularly distinguished automobiles until the colorful Errett Lobban Cord took over the organization. Cord was hired as general manager in 1924, became vice-president the following year, and was then made president in 1926.

A fast-moving salesman, promoter and organizer, E. L. Cord claimed to have made and lost $50,000 three times before he was twenty-one. Before coming to Auburn, for example, Cord had arrived in Chicago with less than fifty dollars to his name, become a car salesman, and done so well that he wound up as general manager and part owner of the automobile agency.

By the time Cord reached Indiana the Auburn company had fallen into financial trouble because

it was not selling many cars; but the hustling "boy wonder" quickly changed all that. Building more attractive cars and then advertising them heavily, Cord multiplied Auburn sales over ten times within five years.

The best Auburn that he made was the next-to-last model to be produced, the 1935 851 Speedster (photo). A long, rakish roadster sporting tear-drop fenders and a racy boat-tail, the 851 Speedster had a supercharged 280-cubic-inch engine. Four flexible chrome-plated exhaust pipes curved downward *outside* the hood on the driver's side; and, unusual for its day, there were no running boards.

Each of the approximately five hundred 851 Speedsters that were sold (all at a loss to the company) had a signed plate on the instrument panel stating that the car had been tested at speed before it left the factory and had exceeded one hundred miles an hour. Since then, however, some critics have complained that these plates were installed before the cars were ever finished.

In 1935, as part of an advertising campaign, an 851 Speedster was taken to the Bonneville Salt Flats in Utah where it set several records for stock cars. Among them was an average speed of 102.9 mph for twelve hours, and an Auburn thus became the first fully equipped U.S. stock car to exceed one hundred mph for so long a time.

Duesenberg (dōoz'-ĕn-bẽrg). Sometimes mistakenly thought of as a German car, the Duesenberg is probably the greatest automobile ever built in the United States. Fred S. Duesenberg was born in Germany, it it true, but he and his younger brother, August, came to Iowa as boys. As young men they first set up as bicycle manufacturers, then later progressed to the building of highly successful racing cars. During World War I they made military engines, including Bugatti aircraft engines under license from Molsheim.

The first Duesenberg passenger car was the Model A, manufactured in Indianapolis, Indiana, from 1921 until 1926 by Fred with Augie's assistance. The expensive Model A, made to the highest mechanical standards, was the first U.S. car to have a straight-eight engine, an overhead camshaft and hydraulic brakes. It did not sell well, however, for the Duesenbergs were not particularly good businessmen; and their company was near financial collapse by 1926.

At that point none other than the energetic E. L. Cord took over financial control of the concern, and it was decided to produce a new model. The result

was the biggest, fastest, best-looking, most advanced, most powerful and most luxurious automobile yet seen in America. Known as the Model J unsupercharged and the SJ when supercharged, it was also the most expensive U.S. car to date, the chassis alone costing as much as ten thousand depression dollars.

Built primarily between 1930 and 1936, the magnificently gigantic J-type Duesenbergs could be purchased by only the very rich. They were widely recognized as the best U.S. automobiles on the road, though; and the still-heard phrase, "It's a doozy," came into the language during the thirties to describe other things of unmatched excellence as well.

Racing Duesenbergs had won the Indianapolis 500 in 1924, 1925 and 1927; and the 420-cubic-inch straight-eight engine of the J cars was based directly on those of the racers. Because of its racing heritage an SJ Duesenberg could reach more than one hundred miles an hour in *second gear* alone and had a top speed of something like one hundred and thirty miles an hour. Each S and SJ chassis was tested for five hundred miles at the Indianapolis Speedway before it went to a U.S. or European coachwork firm for the glamorous body that could increase its price by as much as another $10,000. The photograph shows a Hubley model of a 1930 SJ.

The Duesenberg was known for the completeness of its instrument panel which even included lights that went on when it was time to change the oil and add water to the battery. In many Deusies this extensive panel was duplicated in the rear seat so the passengers could also keep track of the car's performance.

Cord. Even though he was already producing the fleet Auburns and mighty Duesenbergs in the late Twenties, Errett Lobban Cord then decided to build another car. It was to cost somewhat more than the Auburn but far less than a Duesenberg, he determined, and it would bear his own name.

The L-29 Cord made its debut in 1929, and like Cord's other cars proved an immediate attention-getter. The sleek, low-lined L-29 used an unusual drive system. At that time, as now, the engines of most automobiles turned the rear wheels to push the cars along; but the engine of the new Cord drove the front wheels directly. This system pulled the car down the road and enabled it to corner better. Unfortunately, the stock-market crash of 1929 occurred only a few months after the introduction of the L-29, and the unconventional car sold poorly in the bleak depression that followed. The L-29 had to be withdrawn from production in 1932.

By 1934 money was so scarce that sales of Auburns and Duesenbergs had slumped to the point that Cord's automotive empire was close to bankruptcy. His characteristic solution was to risk everything on one last revolutionary model, the 810 Cord, and that gamble almost worked.

The new car created a sensation wherever it was exhibited, partly because of the front-wheel drive carried over from the L-29 but mostly because of the 810's styling that was years ahead of its time. Even as late as 1952, seventeen years later, the Museum of Modern Art in New York City chose the 810 as one of the ten best examples of industrial styling to be found. Almost shockingly modernistic for 1936, the 810 Cord had a flat, horizontally ribbed wrap-around "coffin-nose," headlights that folded back into tear-drop fenders, and such advanced details as flush-mounted taillights and a concealed gas cap.

A variation of the 810 Cord, the 812 (photo), featuring an optional supercharger, was offered for 1937; but the days of Auburn-Cord-Duesenberg were already numbered. The 810 was publicly shown before enough cars had been made to meet the demand that was aroused; and the haste to catch up on production afterwards allowed a number of 810's with faults to be sold. This mistake had a bad

effect on further sales; and, in combination with the continuing financial crisis, became the last straw for Cord's organization. Auburn-Cord-Duesenberg made its last car in 1937.

Stutz. Harry C. Stutz manufactured both racing and passenger cars in Indianapolis, Indiana, beginning in 1911. He entered the very first Stutz that was completed in the inaugural Indianapolis 500 to gain publicity; and when the brand-new automobile finished eleventh, he coined the famous Stutz slogan, "The Car That Made Good in a Day."

Best known of the early street Stutz's was a pioneer sports car called the Stutz Bearcat, first made in 1914. The popular Bearcat had big wooden wheels and a stripped chassis that carried only fenders, hooded engine and the steering wheel, plus a pair of bucket seats with the cylindrical gas tank strapped on behind. There was no body as such at all.

In 1919 Harry C. Stutz established a second organization to manufacture a new car (named HCS with his initials), selling his interest in the original company to others who continued to produce Stutz automobiles. Frederick E. Moskovics eventually became the new president of Stutz; and in 1926 the first of a series of European-style, straight-eight

Stutzes was introduced. Swift, very well made cars of progressive design, they were much lower than other U.S. automobiles of their class.

The boat-tailed speedster model, usually painted black, was called the Black Hawk; and in 1928 a Stutz Black Hawk nearly ended the Bentley domination of the Le Mans twenty-four-hour race in France. A single, privately owned Black Hawk battled a factory team of three Bentleys on their own terms, even leading the long race until dawn, but finally finished second to one of them. In this country Auburn and Stutz were arch racing rivals, and they met in 1928 at Daytona Beach to settle

which made the faster U.S. stock car. In the confrontation on the hard-packed Florida sand, a Black Hawk averaged 106.5 mph to an Auburn Speedster's 104.3.

Later that spring the famous challenge race between a Black Hawk and an Hispano-Suiza H6c took place at the Indianapolis Speedway. Moskovics had bet $25,000 that the more agile Stutz could beat the larger Hisso "Boulogne" in a twenty-four-hour race, but lost his money when the engine of the Black Hawk failed. (The winning H6c is shown in the photograph on page 19.)

The Stutz most respected by collectors is the DV-32, built from 1931 until the company ceased operations in 1935. Its straight-eight, 322-cubic-inch engine had four valves for each cylinder instead of the usual two, "DV" standing for "Dual Valves" and "32" for their total number. There were also twin overhead camshafts to open and close the valves, another advanced feature for the time.

The "Bearcat" name was revived for sporting versions of the DV-32, which had two-seater bodies on special shortened chassis. A small number of Super Bearcats (photo) were even shorter, lighter and faster.

Packard. As Henry Royce was also to do five years later, James W. Packard decided to build his own automobile when the one he bought kept breaking down. He and his brother William completed the first Packard in 1899; and like the other cars of that time it pretty much resembled a carriage without its horse.

But unlike most other horseless carriages the one-cylinder, twelve-horsepower Model A Packard was sturdy and reliable; and after it had been put into production it sold very well. In 1901 Packard became the first U.S. car to have a steering wheel instead of the usual lever; then in 1903 the plant was moved from Warren, Ohio (where Packard had originally been a manufacturer of electrical supplies), to Detroit.

By the time James Packard retired as company president in 1909, the Packard had become a four-cylinder car. After his departure the firm continued to turn out high-quality automobiles of progressive design, introducing a six-cylinder model in 1911 which was followed, in 1915, by the "Twin Six," the first production twelve-cylinder car in the country. A Packard of that period could be recognized by the red hexagons indented in its hubcaps plus the yoke-shaped top of its radiator; and traces of these lines could still be seen in the styling of Packards many years later.

The basic Packard engine during the twenties and thirties was a straight eight, handsome custom-bodied Packard Eights being among the most prestigious cars of the day. But from 1932 (photo) until 1939 Packard also made big V-12 engines again, and the beautiful giants with these large power plants have become the most prized Packards of all.

Enthusiasts have often argued the merits of these large Packards as compared to those of the

more costly European classics. Even if the edge in craftmanship *is* given to the Europeans, it must be remembered that the Packard was basically a mass-produced automobile, 5,744 Packard Twelves being made as compared to only thirty 8B Isotta-Fraschinis, for example. And, after all, it was a great accomplishment for the quality of a far less expensive, essentially production-line car to approach that of a hand-built special. In any case experts consider the Packard Eights and Twelves of the twenties and thirties to meet all the other requirements for being classics and make an exception of their origin.

In 1935 Packard started making a much smaller and cheaper automobile in an attempt to survive the depression, and the company limped along building conventional cars until 1958 when it finally collapsed. It is the classic models that Packard fanciers prefer to remember, however, for they were the cars that deserved the company's famous slogan (said to originate when someone wrote James Packard for a sales pamphlet), "Ask the Man Who Owns One."

Cadillac. While today's Cadillacs are large and luxurious in comparison to most other automobiles, time and circumstances have diminished the reputation earned by the classic Cadillacs of the thirties. Status symbol that the modern Caddie is, those who admire classic cars do not consider it to be the equal of its older relative in quality, engineering or appearance.

The earliest Cadillacs, first built in 1902, were tiny automobiles with one-cylinder engines that were manufactured by Henry M. Leland, a former machine-tool maker. They were named after Antoine de la Mothe Cadillac, the French governor of the territory of Louisiana who established Detroit, where Cadillacs have always been built, in 1701.

Leland, who became general manager of Cadillac in 1904, was one of the first to build cars from standard interchangeable parts instead of the hand-fitted individually sized pieces used previously. In 1908 his company won the English Dewar Trophy for a demonstration in which three Cadillacs were completely stripped, the parts shuffled, and then put back together again. Each of the three scrambled cars then completed five hundred miles around a race track with no trouble.

Leland's firm was taken over by the growing giant of General Motors the following year, and in 1913 the reorganized company won the Dewar

Trophy again, this time for building the first car to have an electric self-starter instead of a dangerous hand crank. Cadillacs were also the first cars to have electric lights as well as the first in the United States to have production V-8 engines.

In 1917 Henry Leland and his son, Wilfred, left Cadillac to build aircraft engines and later began work on another luxury car, the Lincoln. The Cadillac division of General Motors made great progress in spite of their loss, however, and produced its most memorable cars in the early thirties. During the classic period there were three series of Cadillacs manufactured, those with a V-8 engine, those with a larger V-12, and the fabulously complicated, gas-guzzling V-16-powered cars.

The mammoth V-16 Cadillac engine was basically two straight eights mounted at a forty-five-degree angle on a common crankcase. Each bank of eight cylinders had its own fuel pump, carburetor, water pump and ignition system, and could be operated independently. Still, in spite of its complexity, the 165-horsepower V-16 was so quiet in operation that the only sound heard at idle was the snap of electrical sparks. Just as strong as it was silent, the V-16 Cadillac engine was able to smoothly accelerate a three-ton car in high gear from a speed as low as just over two miles an hour to nearly one hundred.

V-16 Cadillacs were in production from 1930 (photo) until 1940, and fifteen fashionable body styles were generally available. As compared to a V-8 Cadillac's price of about $3,000 a V-16 could cost as much as $10,000.

Lincoln Continental. When Henry Leland and his son Wilfred left Cadillac to set up their own company in 1917, they first manufactured engines for the military aircraft of World War I. It was 1920 before they were able to produce their first automobile, which Henry Leland named for Abraham Lincoln.

The Leland Lincolns were big and costly cars of high quality; and in accordance with Henry's many posted signs of "Craftsmanship a Creed, Accuracy a Law," they were constructed with the greatest precision. Their body styling was so boxily unattractive, however, that sales were slow; and before long the firm was badly in the red. Then in 1922 Henry Ford bought the struggling concern and made it a division of his company.

Henry's son, Edsel Ford, was president of the Ford Motor Company by then and under his direction the quality of the Lincoln was strictly maintained. In addition the car's appearance and performance were much improved, and sales quickly increased. Because they were so well made and so reliable Lincolns were owned by U.S. Presidents of the time; and because of their speed they were also the favorite of gangsters and pursuing police alike during the Prohibition years.

When the depression of the thirties caused the demand for the expensive Lincolns to shrink, a medium-priced model, the Lincoln Zephyr, was placed on the market. One of the first U.S. production cars to have its frame and body built as a single unit, the 1936 V-12 Lincoln Zephyr was also the first U.S. car to be successfully streamlined.

Edsel Ford, whose primary interest was automotive styling, had the Lincoln design department work out a special convertible coupe for him in 1938 that was based on a Zephyr chassis. He had just returned from a vacation in Europe at the time, and he told his designers that he wanted the car to look "strictly continental." A particular feature upon which he insisted, even though others disagreed at first, was the car's rear-mounted, exposed spare wheel. His idea eventually proved to be one of the strongest elements of the final design.

While Edsel's "special" was not unusual mechanically, its European-style lines were so appealing that the car (photo) caused great excitement wherever he went; and many people wanted to order a duplicate as soon as they saw it. Consequently the Continental was put into limited production for the 1940 model year in both convertible and hardtop coupe forms.

But manufacture of the Continental had to be suspended in 1942 because of World War II. And then, even though production was resumed after

the war, the car's future was still in doubt because of the increasingly expensive hand work involved. Unable to be mass-produced, the Lincoln Continental was eventually dropped in 1948 after only six years of life. Although the Ford Motor Company has used the name again since then, experts favor the original Continental and consider it to be "the last of the classics."

CAR	BUILT	WHEELBASE IN INCHES	CHASSIS WEIGHT IN POUNDS
Bugatti 57SC	1936-38 France	117	2,100
Hispano-Suiza H6	1928-31 France	133	2,500
Mercedes-Benz SSKL	1931-33 Germany	116	2,250
Rolls-Royce Continental Phantom II	1932-35 Great Britain	144	3,750
4.5 Blower Bentley	1927-31 Great Britain	130	2,800
Alfa Romeo 1750GS	1929-34 Italy	108	2,000 with body
Isotta-Fraschini 8B	1931-36 Italy	134 or 145	3,750
Auburn 851 Speedster	1935 U.S.	127	3,700 with body
Duesenberg SJ	1932-37 U.S.	143	5,200 with body
Cord 812	1937 U.S.	125	3,500 with body
Stutz DV-32 Bearcat	1931-35 U.S.	135	4,895 with body
Packard V-12	1932-39 U.S.	139 or 144	6,000 with body
Cadillac V-16	1930-40 U.S.	148	6,000 with body
Lincoln Continental	1940-42, 1946-48 U.S.	125	3,890 with body
For comparison:			
Chevrolet Impala	1973 U.S.	122	4,435 with body

CYLINDERS	SIZE OF ENGINE IN CUBIC INCHES	HORSE-POWER	APPROXIMATE TOP SPEED IN MILES PER HOUR
Straight 8	199 supercharged	200	130
Straight 6	480	200	100
Straight 6	428 supercharged	300	130
Straight 6	468	company does not release	100
Straight 4	268 supercharged	240	125
Straight 6	107 supercharged	85	95
Straight 8	450	150	90
Straight 8	280 supercharged	150	104
Straight 8	420 supercharged	320	130
V-8	289 supercharged	195	110
Straight 8	322	156	105
V-12	473	175	85
V-16	452	165	100
V-12	292	120	90
V-8	350	145	95

4 / Seeing Classic Cars

CLASSIC CARS, rare to begin with because so few were made, have become even scarcer over the years, a number having disappeared with the passage of time. Collectors have searched out as many as possible, meticulously restoring them to showroom condition; but by now the chances of finding further unknown examples are quite slim. The days when an Isotta-Fraschini could be turned up in a forgotten corner of a junkyard or an abandoned Cord found in an old garage are just about gone at this point.

And while the total number of classic cars still in existence is relatively small (ten thousand or so in the U.S. according to the CCCA), interest in them has increased greatly recently. Thus the few classics that do change hands from time to time are sold for ever-increasing amounts; and prices have become so high that even the rich original owners of the automobiles might be shocked.

Because they are so rare and so expensive, classic cars are not apt to be seen in the parking lot of your neighborhood supermarket. There have been a few attempts at building modern replicas of classic coachwork on present-day chassis, such as plastic-bodied Cords and Auburns and the Excalibur SS which is an imitation Mercedes SSK; and you may spot one of these "replicars" on the road occasionally, it is true. They are not to be confused with the real thing, though, which are best seen in museums or at special outdoor shows.

A number of automotive museums have now been established in the United States, most of them specializing in older antique cars; but several exhibit classic cars as well. Largest of all is Harrah's Automobile Collection in Reno, Nevada, which displays over one thousand cars at a time. Among their many classics are no less than seventeen Rolls-Royces and two dozen Stutzes, for instance.

Much smaller, but a most distinguished collection, particularly of foreign classics, is the Briggs

Cunningham Automotive Museum, 250 Baker Street, Costa Mesa, California. Included in the classics there are a rare SSJ Duesenberg and the H6c Hispano-Suiza that beat the Stutz at Indianapolis.

Other good museums that feature classic cars are the Museum of Automobiles, Route 3, Morrilton, Arkansas; the Frederick C. Crawford Auto-Aviation Museum, 10825 East Boulevard, Cleveland, Ohio; and the Early American Museum in Silver Springs, Florida.

Many smaller museums are scattered throughout the country, too, not to mention numerous private collections that are often open to the public. Then there are the many individual owners of classic cars who periodically meet for outdoor competitions (frequently in association with antique car owners) during which their automobiles are judged for the beauty and authenticity of their restoration.

With the exception of CCCA events the public is usually admitted to these meetings, and attending one is just about the best way of getting a close-up look at some of these marvelous old cars. Local librarians can help find out when such shows are scheduled in your area. One good source is the

Many outdoor exhibitions of classic cars are held each year, usually in association with antique automobile meets. The light-colored car is a 1924 H6 Hispano-Suiza.

"Collectors' Calendar" in a newspaper called *Autoweek*. Even more complete listings can be found in *Hemmings Motor News* and *Old Cars*, but these newspapers are usually harder to locate.

Whenever you do have a chance to see classic cars, keep their rarity and value in mind. The basic rule for classic car watching is always: Don't Touch! Owners are nearly always pleased to answer questions about their vehicles—some even give rides at outdoor shows—but they most definitely do not appreciate finger marks, pressure on body panels

The basic rule for classic car watching is always: Don't Touch!

to see how strong they are, or anything else of the sort.

If you are not able to visit a museum or go to a show, another way of learning a great deal about classic cars is to build some of the excellent model kits that are now widely available, gradually assembling your own miniature museum. Monogram Models, for instance, has a good series of classic cars in 1/24 scale, including a 1931 Rolls-Royce Phantom II, a 1934 Duesenberg SJ, a 1937 Cord 812 and a 1941 Lincoln Continental. Monogram kits consist of plastic parts to be glued together, and they do not require painting (except for such details as door handles and taillights) if you like their choice of color. They cost about $3.50 each.

Johan Models makes a 1931 V-16 Cadillac in 1/25 scale which goes together in a similar way, although there are more parts for greater detail. There is a choice of three different body styles at around two dollars or so. As with the Monogram kits painting is not absolutely required, but if carefully done it will improve the looks of your Cadillac considerably.

The 1/25-scale classic car kits of Life-Like Products, Inc., relatively simple to build and priced at about two dollars each, are good projects for beginning modelers to try. Life-Like currently lists a Lincoln-Continental, an 812 Cord and an Auburn Speedster, and it is likely that other cars will be added to the series in the future.

Larger, more detailed and more expensive than any of the preceding are the Hubley kits. They contain as many as one hundred and fifty parts, most of them metal, which require the filing away of considerable scrap as well as painting. Beautiful models for more experienced builders, a 1/18 SJ Duesenberg (choice of two body styles) sells for about twelve dollars (see photo, page 38) and a 1/22 1930 Packard (three body styles available) is around eight dollars.

Even bigger and more detailed is the 1/12 scale Model Products Blower Bentley. This kit, which sells for about ten dollars, consists of more than 275 plastic parts, many of them plated. When completed the handsome and highly accurate model is almost fifteen inches long and only painting of a few small details is strictly necessary.

By far the most complex, most difficult and most expensive of all the classic car kits is — fittingly enough — a 1/8 scale Rolls-Royce Phantom II coupe from the Pocher company in Italy. The ultimate kit, it contains over two thousand separate pieces, most

The chassis of Model Products' highly detailed 4.5 Blower Bentley. The kit contains more than 275 parts and the finished car is almost fifteen inches long. Note the supercharger in front of the radiator.

of which are to be assembled with tiny bolts and nuts; and when completed the model's engine, steering, suspension and brakes all work like the real thing. The local hobby shop may not have one though, for availability is very limited. Then, too, there is the matter of price — the kit lists at $189.50, and assembled the model costs a staggering $985.50!

INDEX

Order of entries: individuals, organizations, models (arranged chronologically), and general references

Page numbers in italics refer to photographs

Abernathy, Bud and Temple, 34
Aircraft engines, Bugatti, 149
Aircraft engines, Hispano-Suiza, 129-130
Aircraft engines, Isotta-Fraschini, 143
Aircraft engines, Leland (Liberty), 163
Alfa Romeo 6C, 140-141
Alfa Romeo 1750, 141-142
Alfa Romeo 1750GS, *141,* 142
American Automobile Association, 89
American Motors Corporation, 45
Anonima Lombarda Fabbrica Automobili (ALFA), 140
Antique Automobile Club of America, 6
Antique cars, appeal, 5
Antique cars, defined, 5-6
Apperson brothers, 29
Auburn Automobile Company, 146, 147, 148

Auburn Speedster, 146, *147,* 148-149, 155-156
Auctions, antique car, *59,* 60

Barber, Amzi L., 79-80, 82
"Beetle." *See* "Wogglebug"
Bentley, W.O., 137
Bentley Three-Liter, 137-138
Bentley "Big Six," 138
Bentley "Speed Six," 138
Bentley 4.5-Liter, 138
Bentley 4.5-Liter, supercharged, 139, *139, 175* (model)
Bentley Eight-Liter, 139
"Bentley Boys," 139
Bentleys racing at Le Mans, France, 138, 155
Benz, Karl, 7, 68, 132
Birkigt, Marc, 129-130
Blitzen Benz, 99
"Blower Bentleys," 138-139, *139, 175* (model)
"Blue Label" Bentleys, 137

177

Bowden, Herbert L., 90-91
Briggs Cunningham Automotive Museum, Costa Mesa, California, 169-170
Briscoe, Benjamin, 27, 30, 35, 37
Briscoe, Frank, 27, 30, 32, 35
Briscoe Motor Company, 35, 37
Briscoe, 35-37, *36*
Brush, Alanson P., 32
Brush Runabout Company, 32
Brush Runabout, 32-34, *33*
"Bug." *See* Bugatti or "Wogglebug"
Bugatti, Ettore, 126-128, 137
Bugatti, Jean, 128
Bugatti 57, 128
Bugatti 57SC "Atlantic" coupe, *127,* 128
Buick, David D., 25-28, 37
Buick Motor Company, 28
Buick, 1912, *27*

Cadillac, Antoine de la Mothe, 160
Cadillac Automobile Company, 39, 46
Cadillac, 1924, *48*
Cadillac V-16, *161,* 162
Cannon, 86
Chapin, Roy D., 13-14, 42, 44-45, 50
Chevrolet, Louis, 38, 40
Chevrolet Motor Company, 40-41
Chevrolet 490, 41
Chevrolet, 1918, *39*

Chevrolet Six, 41, 55
Chevrolet-Ford sales rivalry, 41
Christie, Walter, 92
Christie, 92-93
Chrysler, Walter P., 31
Chrysler Corporation, 31
Classic Car Club of America, 120, 125
Classic cars, appearance, 123
Classic cars, coachwork, 123-125
Classic cars, compared statistically, 166-167
Classic cars, cost, 125
Classic cars, defined, 120-121
Coffin, Howard, 42-43
Cord, Errett Lobham, 146-148, 149, 151, 152, 154
Cord L-29, 152
Cord 810, 152-153
Cord 812, 153, *153*
Crankshaft, Hispano-Suiza, 130
Crankshaft, Hudson, 43-44
Cugnot, Nicolas, 67
Curved-dash Oldsmobile, *11,* 12-13

Daimler, Gottlieb, 7, 132
Daimler-Benz, 132
Dewar Trophy, 47, 160-161
Doble, 112
Dodge, John and Horace, 19
Duesenberg, August, 149
Duesenberg, Fred S., 149
Duesenberg Model A, 149

Duesenberg J-types, 60, 150-151; SJ, *150* (model)
Durant, William C., 28, 38-42, 47
Durbin, Frank, 84-85, *85*, 96
Duryea, Charles E., 7-8, 10, 68
Duryea, J. Frank, 7-10, 68
Duryea Motor Wagon Company, 10
Duryea, 1893, 8-10, *9*, 56

E.M.F. *See* Everitt-Metzger-Flanders Company
E.M.F. Thirty, 24-25, *24*
Engines, classic cars, 21-22
Essex, 44-45
Evans, Oliver, 67
Everitt, B.F., 23
Everitt-Metzger-Flanders Company, 23-25

Ferrari, Enzio, 140
Fiat, 91
Flanders, Walter E., 23, 31
Flanders, 24
Flying Dutchman II, 90-91
Ford, Edsel, 163, 164
Ford, Henry, 17-19, 20, 21, 22, 23, 26, 39, 52, 53, 89, 90, 110, 145, 163
Ford Motor Company, 19, 20, 90, 163
Ford "Quadricycle," 18, 56
Ford Arrow, 89
Ford Models A-S, 19-20

Ford Model T, 17, *18,* 20-22
Ford Model A, 52-55, *54*
Ford-Chevrolet sales rivalry, 41
Fraschini, Vincenzo, 142

General Motors Company, 38, 40, 41, 47, 160, 161
Glidden, Charles J., 30
Glidden Tours, 30-31
"Green Label" Bentleys, 138
Grout, 86

Harrah's Automobile Collection, Reno, Nevada, 57, 169
Haynes, Elwood, 28-29
Haynes, 28, 56
Henry Ford Company, 46
Henry Ford Museum, Dearborn, Michigan, 56
Hispano-Suiza "Alfonso," 129
Hispano-Suiza H6, 130-131
Hispano-Suiza H6b town car, *124*
Hispano-Suiza H6c "Boulogne," 130, *131,* 156
Hispano-Suiza Type 68, 131
Hispano-Suiza aircraft engines, 129-130
Hispano-Suiza leakage test, 121-122
Hudson, J.L., 43
Hudson Motor Car Company, 43, 45
Hudson Six, *43*

Indianapolis 500, 154
Indianapolis Speedway, 156
Isotta, Cesare, 142
Isotta-Fraschini, Tipo 8, 143
Isotta-Fraschini, Tipo 8A, 144, *144;* 8A engine *122*
Isotta-Fraschini, Tipo 8B, 144
Isotta-Fraschini aircraft engines, 143

Jano, Vittorio, 140-141
Joy, Henry B., 50

"Le Patron." *See* Bugatti, Ettore
Leland, Henry, 45-47, 160-161, 162-163
Leland, Wilfred, 46, 47, 161, 162
Le Mans, France, twenty-four-hour race, 139, 155
Lincoln, 47, 163
Lincoln Continental, 164-165, *165*
Lincoln Zephyr, 163-164
Little Motor Car Company, 40
Locomobile Company of America, 80-83
Locomobile, 1899 advertisement, *81*

Macdonald, Arthur, 90
Marriott, Fred H., 17, 71, 91-99, *94, 95, 97, 98*
Mason Motor Car Company, 40

Maxwell, Jonathan D., 29-31
Maxwell, 1911, *29*
Maxwell-Briscoe, 30
Mercedes Ninety, 90
Mercedes Model K, 133
Mercedes, S series, 132-134
Mercedes SS, SSK, SSKL, 134; SSK, *133*
Mercedes-Benz, 132-134
Metzger, William, 23-24
"Merry Oldsmobile," *11,* 12-13
Mobile Company of America, 80, 82, 83
Models, classic car, 173-175
Mors, 89
Moskovics, Frederick E., 154, 156
Museums, antique car, listed by state, 61-62
Museums, classic car, 169-170

Napier, 90, 91
Nash Motor Company, 45
New York-to-Paris race, 1908, 42

Oakland, 32, 39
Ohio. *See* Packard Model A.
Old Pacific, 50-51, 56
Oldfield, Barney, 87, 99
Olds, Ransom E., 10-12, 13, 14, 45
Olds Motor Works, 12, 38, 42
Oldsmobile, curved-dash, *11,* 12-14

Ormond Beach, Florida, 17, 21, 51, 88-99

Packard, James W., 48-49, 50, 157, 159
Packard, William, 49, 157
Packard Model A, 49, 157
Packard Model C, 49, 50
Packard Twin-Six, 51, 157, 158
Packard Eight, *51,* 158
Packard Twelve, 158, *158*
Pierce-Arrow, 31
Plymouth, 34
Porsche, Ferdinand, 132-133

"Quadricycle" (Ford), 18

Reo, 14
"Red Label" Bentleys, 137
"Replicars," 169
Rolls, Charles, 135
Rolls-Royce Ltd., 135, 139
Rolls-Royce Silver Ghost, 136
Rolls-Royce Phantom I, 136
Rolls-Royce Phantom II, 136
Rolls-Royce Phantom II Continental, 136-137, *136*
Romeo, Nicola, 140
Roper, Sylvester H., 68
Ross, Louis S., 90
Royce, Henry, 135

Serpollet, 89
Shows, antique car, 3-4, 58-60
Shows, classic car, 170-173
Silent Northern, 29, 31
Sloan Museum, Flint, Michigan, 56-57
Smithsonian Institution, Washington, D.C., 56
Stanley, Francis Edgar, 15-16, 65-67, 69-73, 76-77, 80, 82, 83, 84, 85, 86, 87, 91, 92, 95, 96, 98, 99, 100, 105, 108, 110-112, *66, 74, 111*
Stanley, Freelan Oscar, 15-16, 65-67, 69-75, 76-80, 82, 83, 100, 105-106, 110-111, 112, *66*
Stanley, Raymond, 84-85, 92-93, 108
Stanley Motor Carriage Company, 16, 73, 105-110
Stanley, original, *66*
Stanley, 1904, *15, 74*
Stanley "Gentlemen's Speedy Roadster," *85,* 100-101, 104
Stanley Mountain Wagon, 83
Stanley boiler, 102, 105-106
Stanley burner, 102, 107, 108
Stanley, driving, 102, 104
Stanley engine, 102, *103*
Stanley photographic plates, 69-70, 82
Stanley, starting, 107
Stork emblem, Hispano-Suiza, 130
Studebaker Brothers Manufacturing Company, 25
Stutz, Harry C., 154

Stutz Bearcat, 154, 156
Stutz Black Hawk, 155-156
Stutz DV-32, 156
Stutz Super Bearcat, *155,* 156
Stutz, Hispano-Suiza challenge race, 156
Stutz racing at Le Mans, France, 155

Terraplane. *See* Essex
Thomas, E.R., 42
Thomas, 42

United States Motor Company, 34-35

Vanderbilt, William K., Jr., 89, 90
Vanderbilt Cup races, 89, 91
Vermont, The, 50-51, 56

Walker, John Brisben, 76-82
White, 112
Williams, Calvin and Charles, 114
Williams, 114-115
Winton, Alexander, 48
"Wogglebug," 16-17, 86-87, 90-99, *87, 94, 95, 97, 98*
World Land Speed Record, 17, 19, 89-90, 93-95, 96-99